DAYTON
COMES of AGE

THE CITY THROUGH THE EYES OF JOHN H. PATTERSON, 1897–1922

CLAUDIA WATSON

MONTGOMERY COUNTY HISTORICAL SOCIETY

THE MONTGOMERY COUNTY HISTORICAL SOCIETY

HAS EXISTED FOR OVER ONE HUNDRED YEARS TO

COLLECT, PRESERVE, INTERPRET, EXHIBIT AND

TEACH THE MIAMI VALLEY'S LEGACY. IT IS A MAJOR

PROMOTER OF COMMUNITY PRIDE AND WILL BE A KEY

ELEMENT OF CONTINUED DOWNTOWN RESURGENCE.

MONTGOMERY COUNTY HISTORICAL SOCIETY

224 NORTH ST. CLAIR STREET

DAYTON, OH 45402

(937) 228-6271

WWW.DAYTONHISTORY.ORG

Published by the Montgomery County Historical Society

ISBN 0-9720965-0-7

This book was made possible in part by funding from NCR,
National City, and the Montgomery County Historical Society Guild

Design: VMA

Printing: Hammer Graphics/Central Printing Company

Paper: MeadWestvaco Signature Dull

C O N T E N T S

Before John H. Patterson and his brother, Frank, bought the National Manufacturing Company on November 22, 1884, and changed its name to The National Cash Register Company, they operated a coal business in Dayton. They ordered coal from the mines and delivered it to their customers in brown wagons with "Patterson and Company" in gold letters on the sides.

Every day a clerk collected the previous day's receipts. Cash was kept in a drawer and change made from it. Nobody kept accounts.

John Patterson put a cash register in his Coalton, Ohio store and his branch offices. He explained that it was only to keep accounts and prevent mistakes. The registers, which he bought from J. H. Eckert, who had bought the business from the inventor, James A. Ritty, had no cash drawers, so the money was still kept in a table drawer.

The first day when the clerk checked the register he found the cash $2 short. When the cash was $2 short the second day, Patterson warned the clerk that the same mistake two days in a row would not be tolerated.

Next day the cash was again $2 short. Patterson went to the branches and punched the $2 key. "There is nothing wrong with this machine," he said. "I want you to check the cash every two hours today. That way we can find out when the money disappears."

At the end of the day the register and the cash agreed. But the next morning the cash was again $2 short. Patterson hired a police officer to watch the office at night.

It was again short. "Who went into that office last night?" Patterson asked the officer.

"Nobody. I watched that office all night. Nobody went in."

"Obviously somebody did. Tonight you be very sure nobody goes into that office. Do not allow anybody to go into the office."

Next morning the cash was $2 short. "Who came into this office last night?" he asked the policeman.

"Nobody. That is, nobody but the night watchman."

Patterson frowned. "We don't have a night watchman."

"But he told me he was the night watchman. He has been for the last five years."

"We did have a night watchman," said Patterson, "but two years ago I fired him and saved his $2 nightly pay. Now tonight when he comes, I want you to arrest him."

The discharged watchman confessed he had collected his $2 pay every night since he had been fired.

Patterson did not press charges because he had not collected the man's keys when he fired him. The cash register caught a loss he never knew about and prevented further losses. Two years later he bought the cash register company.

Physically he was not prepossessing. Stanley C. Allyn, his business associate for many years, described him as a small man, standing five feet eight inches and weighing about 150 pounds. "With his sandy hair parted in the middle as a crown to a face notable for inquisitive steely blue eyes set behind dramatic pince-nez glasses," Allyn wrote, "with bushy trimmed eyebrows and a mustache of the English guards type, he looked like an actor made up for the role of a somewhat comic jumping jack.... Surprising to me was his voice, which was high-pitched, edged with irascibility, often downright squeaky."

The business got off to a rocky start.

A $50,000 shipment to England was returned because the machines were defective. Patterson did not understand. He bought the best materials. Why were the machines defective?

He moved his desk into the factory, working under the same conditions as his employees. His men worked for a pittance, and the factory was damp, dirty and dark. He decided the machines broke down because the men had no pride in their company. What did they care whether they did good work or not? "I don't blame these men for doing poor work," he said. "Even I, who own the business, could not perform in these conditions."

He cleaned up the plant, installed rest rooms, added showers and encouraged the employees to bathe on company time. He built an employee cafeteria and served wholesome meals at modest prices. He hired the Olmsted Brothers of Boston to create park-like lawns around new buildings. When the new buildings were completed, they lay on sunny, landscaped grounds which the employees were encouraged to use.

The hub of The National Cash Register Company was the Bulletin Room. It was the center for the communication of Patterson's ideas. They tumbled from him at all hours, a freshet of creativity that often became a deluge. Every inch of wall space was covered with newspaper-page sized messages in large type with the most important messages in red.

He became fascinated with the growth of the city and had his photographers take thousands of pictures in all parts of it, the wealthy environs as well as the poor sections. These photographs, printed from glass plate negatives, give a portrait of the town and represent a living history of Dayton people and their activities.

The NCR Archive has more than 1.5 million images, including 100,000 glass plate negatives and 68,000 glass lantern slides. There are also more than 350 wood and brass cash registers; tens of thousands of engineering drawings of NCR inventions; and more than 1,000 items from the 1913 flood, including photographs, albums, a flood boat replica, and correspondence. The Archive even includes the factory whistle that used to be blown when the work day ended and whenever Patterson wanted all employees to drop their work and go to the windows to welcome him back from a trip.

Not including the brass spittoons. One morning William Blake Patterson (no relation to John Patterson) looked up from his desk in his shop, the Patterson Tool and Supply Company on Third Street near St. Clair, and saw John Patterson sitting on his horse in front of his shop.

He hurried out to the curb. "Good morning, Mr. Patterson. What can I do for you?"

"I want twelve solid brass spittoons for the use of tobacco chewers in my factory. I do not approve of tobacco in any form, but I can't have filthy floors in my plant. Can you get them for me?"

"Oh, yes, certainly. But in solid brass they will cost you a pretty penny."

"Price is no object," Patterson said. "Deliver them as soon as possible. Good day to you." He rode off.

During World War II Mary Louise Patterson, William Blake Patterson's daughter, worked beside a grinding machine in the factory and reported that the spittoons were still in use. One employee spent his entire working career at NCR cleaning and polishing those spittoons.

The brass spittoons have not turned up in the Archive. Where are they?

The incredible resource of this Archive deserves to be supported by the public. It will cost millions to preserve just the photographs that give a living history of every activity in this city. This book, which you hold in your hands, is a sample of the endless wealth in the NCR Archive.

John Patterson went out in the glory of the spotlight as he had lived in it. He loved parades. He died May 7, 1922 on a train as it was nearing Atlantic City. His funeral was a private one, with the Reverend Phil Porter of Christ Episcopal Church reading the simple Episcopal service.

The entire town closed down. High schools and the University of Dayton closed; elementary schools closed for half a day. Businesses closed, flags flew at half-staff, and streetcars stopped for five minutes between 11:45 and 11:50. The front page of the Dayton Daily News, May 9, 1922, carried only the portrait of Patterson and a short poem. Representing every school from Dayton, 1,500 students lined the curbs of both sides of Woodland Avenue to the gates of the cemetery, strewing flowers as the hearse passed by.

He would have liked that.

ROZ YOUNG

Since the fall of 1998, I have had the pleasure of working with the NCR Archive, one of the finest corporate collections in the nation. After four years I am still discovering the many faces of this remarkable collection of over three million items. It is an extraordinary treasure covering a wide range of subjects, and contains every kind of artifact from cash registers to computers and flood boats to factory whistles. The heart of this collection is the 1.5 million images produced by the NCR Photograph Department from the mid-1890s to the present, including 100,000 glass plate negatives from the era of company founder John H. Patterson. Without his intense interest in the city and his belief in the power of photography as a tool to effect change, we would not have the incredible imagery presented in this volume.

I especially want to thank Bill West, NCR Archivist Emeritus, who has always been deeply committed to ensuring that the Archive was preserved as a community legacy. Others at NCR who worked tirelessly to bring about the partnership between NCR and the Historical Society include Mary Karr, Jon Hoak, Doug Foote and CEO Lars Nyberg. Brian Hackett, Executive Director of the Historical Society, had the vision to recognize the importance of the Archive to the community, and the willingness to take on the weighty, but worthwhile, task of caring for the collection. The Historical Society's Board of Trustees has consistently met the challenges that come with such a vast and valuable legacy.

Without our funders the book would not have been possible. I would like to thank NCR, National City and the Montgomery County Historical Society Guild for their generous sponsorship of the publication. I would also like to thank the Allyn Foundation for generously providing funding needed to preserve and digitize many of these remarkable photographs.

I would particularly like to acknowledge Kristina Nyberg, who suggested the project and has given it her warm support. I also owe a debt of gratitude to the Historical Society's Curator Mary Oliver, NCR Archivist Jeff Opt, MCHS trustee Ron Rollins and my father-in-law, Bernard Watson, for editing and proofing the manuscript. Roz Young generously wrote the foreword, and lent her enthusiasm and love of history to the project. Jim Butler, President of the Board of Trustees, has been a constant supporter and has helped in so many ways to make the book a reality.

Thanks to VMA, especially Al Hidalgo, who created the design, and Kenneth Botts, who helped with production issues. I would especially like to thank Curt Dalton, the Historical Society's Curator of Visual Resources, who has contributed greatly to the quality of the book. His careful production of the photographic plates, including scanning and creation of the duotones, allows the reader to view the images at their very best. A very special thanks to my husband, Michael, for his willingness to read and re-read the manuscript, and for his valuable input and constant encouragement. Lastly, thanks to my children, Christiana and Graham, for their patience with the many hours it took to complete the project and for their continual support.

CLAUDIA WATSON

Research Center Director

Montgomery County Historical Society

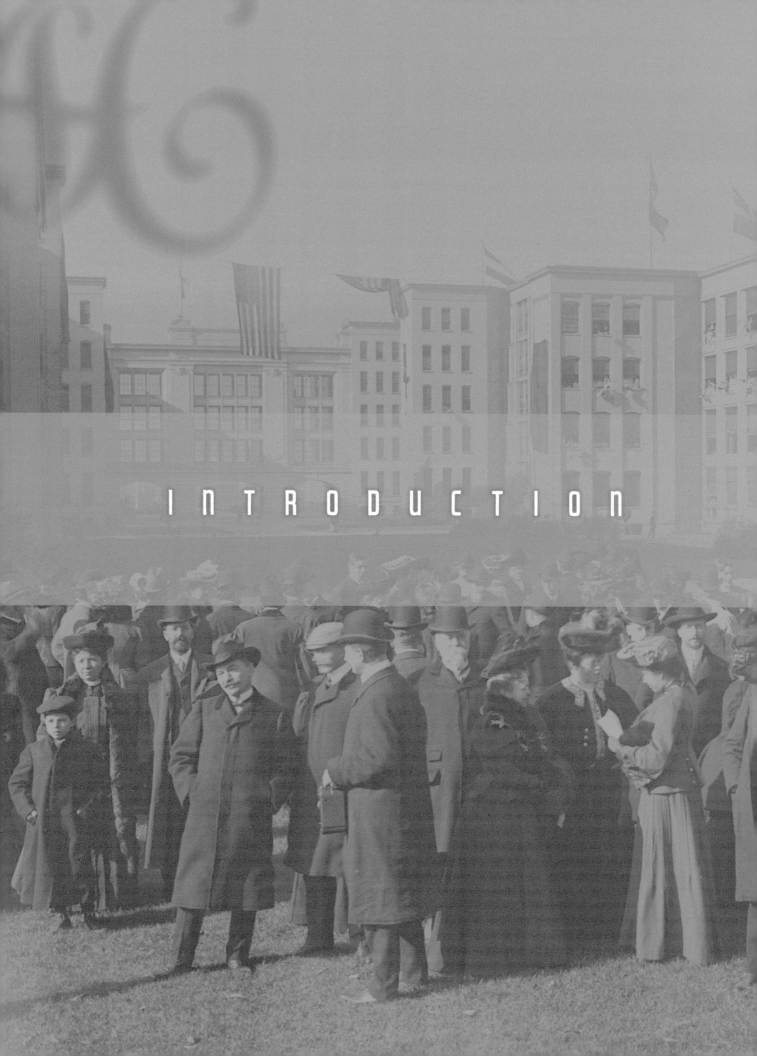

INTRODUCTION

The American people are progressing through inventions.
To handicap the spirit of invention is to handicap the progress of the world.

JOHN H. PATTERSON

It is pretty hard for us to even propose anything here in Dayton without its
attracting the attention of the country generally.
Dayton is the best-advertised city in the nation—and the advertising is generally
all of a favorable nature. That is why it is so important that we make no mistakes.
Other cities might make mistakes and get away with them, but Dayton, before the
world at all times, and looked to for inspiration by many other communities, cannot afford
to have it flashed all over the earth that she has made a mistake.

DAYTON DAILY NEWS, FEBRUARY 25, 1915

Despite the proud words of a local newspaper editor, it has often been said that Dayton has always had an identity problem. For one hundred years, Daytonians have tended to turn a blind eye to the fact that some of the world's life-changing inventions came from what is still sometimes referred to as "America's biggest small town." In 1905 (after Paul Laurence Dunbar had attained international renown, the Wright brothers had invented powered flight and John H. Patterson had created the "model factory of the world"), the Honorable William G. Frizell, speaking to the local Horticultural Society, gave voice to this bland Midwestern identity. Dayton, he said, was not distinguished as a literary center, as were Cincinnati, Cleveland or Columbus. It was not a political center for Daytonians had never held important offices of state. Neither was Dayton distinguished for her famous citizens as Dayton had "not been the birthplace or burial place of many of the great men and women who have made Ohio famous." Indeed, Dayton's only claim to fame, he proclaimed, was as a "model city of attractive homes."

In that period, however, one might have been able to excuse Daytonians' self-dismissal because their self-image had not kept pace with the city's rate of change. Dayton was still in the process of "becoming"—of entering a golden age when it would be known as a center of invention and as a national model of progressive thought and ideals.

Only a little while before, Dayton had been a quiet county seat, a modestly successful commercial center with numerous solid industries. Pictures of Dayton taken in the 1870s and 1880s show a peaceful town, with wide and almost empty streets, where a few horses dozed lazily at hitching posts and isolated buggies and wagons trundled up and down city thoroughfares, offering little competition to the slow-moving horse-drawn streetcars. Streets were either muddy or dusty, depending on the weather, and there was little concern about the rubbish that adorned the city or the hoards of flies which routinely joined families, rich and poor, at mealtime.

Dayton was tired of being a sleepy little town, however; it aspired to greater things, and the growth of cities in general and Dayton's circumstances in particular thrust it forward into a period of spectacular growth. In 1880, the population was 36,678. In 1900, it was 85,333. By 1907, it had reached 140,000.

Not only did the population grow, but the city itself took on some of the trappings of a sophisticated urban center. The town's leading citizens, tired of wading in ankle-deep mud, took elected officials to task in 1889. They organized the Committee of One Hundred, which pushed through the paving of streets, the installation of sewers, and the development of green spaces. By 1900, the day of the large department store had arrived, offering a generous selection of goods to a public long used to suffering from product deprivation and making downtown the destination of a growing number of shoppers. Tall office buildings transformed the skyline, swelling the numbers who came to work in the developing central business district with the result that it took on a bustle unknown to earlier generations. The noise level rose with the activity level; streetcars were said to have been so loud at Third and Main that people couldn't hear themselves think. The sound of horses' hooves, the creak of wagons and the clatter of streetcars combined, especially after 1905, with the sounds of the automobile to create the busy downtown noises of the new century.

The city's industries were changing, too. Dayton had always had a healthy, diverse industrial base, which included the huge Barney and Smith Car Works and large agricultural machining concerns. The turn of the century saw the transformation of city industries, as new products appeared, many of which changed the American way of life. By 1917, Dayton boasted that the city led in the production of airless automobile tires; cash registers; automobile lighting, starting and ignition systems; computing scales; airplanes and aeronautical research and development; sewing machines; golf clubs; electric plants for homes and farms; and many other products.

Dayton soon found that its schools no longer met the new city's needs. Its high-precision industries demanded a well-trained, well-educated population who could read and write and who possessed expertise in mechanical drawing, accounting and the trades. In addition, housekeeping skills became a part of the new domestic science, with schools teaching principles of cooking and cleaning to the upcoming generation of modern house-keepers. With a more prosperous and better-educated population, Art

DAYTON'S BUSIEST CORNER AT THIRD AND MAIN STREETS. THE CALLAHAN BUILDING, THE CITY'S FIRST SKYSCRAPER ERECTED IN 1892, IS AT CENTER.

(with a capital "A") began to be valued for art's sake, and music and art became an accepted part of the curriculum. Teachers were expected to receive formal training in modern methods of instruction, and students were assigned to classes according to grade. Kindergarten, playgrounds, adult classes, and manual training all became a part of the system of public education, establishing the form and structure we know today.

RESCUE WORKERS
BRING FLOOD VICTIMS
TO SAFETY USING
A BOAT MANUFACTURED BY NCR.
BOMBERGER PARK IS IN THE BACKGROUND.

The Great Flood of 1913 was a critical time for the city, an immense disaster which many feared would end Dayton's climb towards greatness. Instead it became Dayton's shining hour, a defining moment that thrust it forward into the brilliant rays of the national spotlight. It was John H. Patterson who stepped in to fill the gap created by the incompetence of the city government. Even before the floodwaters broke through the levees on Tuesday morning, March 25, he halted work at the factory, diverting the massive resources of The National Cash Register Company to rescue and relief work. In typical Patterson style, he applied his brilliant organizational skills to the emergency, saving thousands of lives through quick and effective action.

In the months that followed, an admiring nation watched as the city cleaned up the muddy mess and cleared away rubble. They saw new buildings, constructed using the latest fireproof construction techniques, rise from the ruins. Dayton's business leaders lost no time raising millions of dollars and setting in motion plans for the Miami Conservancy District, an innovative system of flood control which ensured not only the physical safety of the community, but also its economic future by making it a safe place for investment.

The flood only reinforced citizens' dissatisfaction with their current mayoral form of local government. Disgusted with city government's inability to handle the flood emergency, Daytonians gave their mayor and city council the boot. In 1914, Dayton became the first mid-sized American city to put in place the commission/manager form of government, again garnering national comment and admiration as Americans across the nation watched the experiment in local government unfold. Using efficient business methods to grow the modern city, the new government set to work devising building codes, enacting health and welfare regulations, and establishing parks. Out of this period of disaster came a sense of pride and confidence never seen in any other period of the city's history. Dayton was sitting on top of the world; it was a city that had finally come of age.

Such dramatic change is borne from extraordinary circumstances and extraordinary people, and Dayton was fortunate to have progressive businessmen with time, energy and money, which they generously invested into the future of the city. The list included such notables as Adam Schantz, Jr., a real estate developer and brewery owner; John Stoddard, president

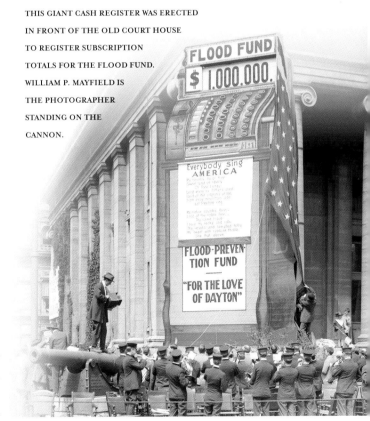

THIS GIANT CASH REGISTER WAS ERECTED
IN FRONT OF THE OLD COURT HOUSE
TO REGISTER SUBSCRIPTION
TOTALS FOR THE FLOOD FUND.
WILLIAM P. MAYFIELD IS
THE PHOTOGRAPHER
STANDING ON THE
CANNON.

of the Stoddard Motor Car Company; H. E. Talbott, an engineer and owner of Dayton's largest construction firm; and Edward Deeds, an NCR executive and financier, and many others. At the forefront of the flurry of activity was John H. Patterson.

Patterson, the energetic, flamboyant and often controversial founder of The National Cash Register Company, or NCR as it is known today, has been called one of the true geniuses of American business. Unfortunately, over the years his fascinating eccentricities have eclipsed the public's memory of his many accomplishments. Patterson's oddities have taken on such a legendary quality that it is difficult to separate fact from fiction. For example, Patterson insisted that his executives become expert horsemen because he believed that only a man who could handle a horse could effectively handle men. This one is fact. Another colorful piece of local lore states that the term "fired," relating to the release of an employee, comes from Patterson's quirky method of indicating dissatisfaction with an employee's performance by placing the unfortunate's desk out on the lawn and setting it on fire. This one is unsubstantiated—not totally unbelievable—but unsubstantiated.

JOHN H. PATTERSON
(FLIP CHART AT HIS SIDE)
ADDRESSING A CLASS OF
NCR SALESMEN AT SUGAR
CAMP. TOM WATSON, SR.
(LATER OF IBM FAME)
IS SEATED AT RIGHT.

The fact is that from the unusual twists and turns of Patterson's mind came innovations in business practices and worker welfare programs that continue to affect how we live and work today. Upon acquiring the cash register company in 1884, he found himself the owner of a business referred to by the Dayton business community as "Phillip's Folly," after the hapless seller of the failing concern. Ignoring his colleagues' predictions of doom, Patterson adopted the "educational advertising" methods of patent medicine salesmen, teaching potential buyers why they needed a cash register and creating a market for the unwanted machine. He oversaw the development of the cash register as a sophisticated data gathering device that revolutionized the retail trade, making the company a pioneer in the development of information technology. Patterson also introduced the practice of systematically training employees when he established the first sales school in 1894. Although employee training is a practice we now view as a matter of common sense, it was seen as downright silly by Patterson's contemporaries and was greatly resisted by his sales force, who believed that a good salesman was born and not made. After NCR continued to thrive even during the severe economic recession of 1893, the business community quit laughing and started copying his "ridiculous" methods.

Perhaps most ridiculed were his extensive worker welfare and civic reform programs. Believing that healthy, well-fed workers were productive workers, he introduced an extensive series of worker welfare programs into the factory, giving NCR the reputation as "the model factory of the world." The spotlessly clean factory buildings, with their 80% glass walls and complete exchange of air every fifteen minutes, were surrounded by carefully manicured grounds designed by the Olmsted Brothers, the architectural landscaping firm who designed New York's Central Park. Employee dining rooms, rest rooms, bathing facilities and medical services helped ensure that NCR employees stayed healthy and productive. Patterson introduced the Suggestion System, in which employees were rewarded for ideas that increased efficiency. A multitude of educational opportunities, including classes on a variety of subjects and a network of clubs and other recreational events, encouraged a feeling of belonging and offered employees the chance to improve their standing within the company. By 1900, hundreds of articles were appearing each year in newspapers and magazines across the world spreading the word about The National Cash Register Company's model manufacturing establishment.

A leading member of the turn of the century Progressive movement, which sought to apply modern methods of efficiency to correcting societal ills, Patterson was also a great believer in the Social Gospel, which stressed Christian responsibility for the welfare of others. Believing poverty and ignorance to be the leading causes of crime and decadence, he promoted education and the development of the child as the best overall methods of prevention and cure for social problems. Like many reformers of the period, he pushed for the professionalization of workers in city government, in teaching and in social work, believing that those trained in the most up-to-date methods were best equipped to address the growing problems in the nation's rapidly expanding cities. Modern and efficient methods of organization had solved the problems of his once floundering business and had made it a success; therefore, he reasoned, organization applied to urban challenges would have the same magical result in the city. Confident in his methods of easing Dayton's growing pains, he set forth his many strong opinions on civic reform, promoting and critiquing his city, bringing about positive change in the community.

COMPANY MEDICAL PERSONNEL PROVIDE AID TO AN INJURED NCR EMPLOYEE, 1904.

Patterson, looking around for an efficient way to communicate his ideas on business and social reform, seized on photography as the most effective method of presenting his ideas. In the end, John Patterson's many innovations in factory organization, business systems and sales, and his determination to bring about massive social change both in cities and the workplace, would combine to create one of the largest and most diverse corporate photographic collections in the world.

Patterson viewed everything he did—from selling to advertising to reform—as simply a matter of teaching, and he fervently believed that information was most effectively imparted by "teaching through the eye." At least 87 percent of what men learned, he claimed, was absorbed through the optic nerve, and he always had a blackboard or flip chart at hand on which he illustrated his points with a scribbled phrase or hastily drawn cartoon. Photography was the perfect tool for Patterson's method of teaching, and improvements in photographic and printing processes, including the acceptance of dry-plate photography, the manufacture of small, simple dry-plate cameras and the advent of the inexpensive halftone reproduction technique, paved the way for the company's extensive use of photography.

From almost the very beginning, Patterson used photographs to document and to teach. Photographs were taken of employees and the factory, of sales conventions and other company events, and of the cash registers themselves. These images were used internally to educate the factory workers and sales agents about each other's work, and were used externally in the multitude of advertising publications designed to increase cash register sales. In the early period, Patterson frequently took the images himself, or hired the services of a professional photographer.

The formal establishment of the NCR Photograph Department resulted from a rather informal encounter between John H. Patterson and a long-time employee, who had worked for Patterson even before the purchase of the company. One day in 1895 Otto Nelson stood contemplating a 6.5″ x 8.5″ camera with lens, plateholders, tripod and other accessories retrieved from a forgotten trunk stowed under a table at NCR. As he began to assemble the equipment, Patterson appeared and, walking briskly over to Nelson, exclaimed in his typical rapid-fire manner, "Whose camera is that? Is it mine? I guess it is, if it came out of that trunk. My, I'm glad you found it. I thought I had lost it in Europe. We're starting a new building tomorrow morning. Take that camera and get a picture of them breaking ground."

With these words, Patterson departed leaving behind a newly appointed company photographer who had never operated a camera before in his life. Nelson knew, however, that in Patterson's mind a lack of knowledge was never an excuse for lack of performance, and he set off to find out how to operate the camera before his date with destiny the next morning. Finally, he asked Alvan Macauley (then head of the NCR Patent Department, later president of the Packard Automobile Company), who was able to quickly provide him with at least the rudimentary knowledge needed to operate the camera.

The next morning Nelson gathered his gear and hurried over to the groundbreaking of the new factory building, carefully applying his newly acquired skills to fulfilling Patterson's request for photos of the event. He then rushed the plates downtown to be developed, and with great relief presented the results to the company president. Patterson was delighted, and instructed him to photograph the progress on the new building twice a week. He also began to request many other images.

At first the photographs were developed by a downtown commercial studio, but the bills for developing and printing grew until one day, Frank Patterson, John's less imaginative brother, called in Nelson to question the exorbitant, seventy-dollar photographic bill for the previous month. After hearing that the photographs were made at John's request, Frank told Nelson to go ahead, but that he would have to learn to develop the pictures himself. A small shed was converted into a darkroom, and the NCR Photograph Department was born.

FIRST NCR
PHOTOGRAPH
DEPARTMENT.

D. H. LORENZ'S
GROCERY,
1203 WAYNE AVENUE.

With the new department comfortably housed on the factory grounds, photography settled in as part of the day-to-day business routine. The amount of work increased exponentially as department staff worked to keep up with the growing demands placed on it by the company president. Patterson had a broad vision for the infinite expansion of the cash register business, and he believed photography was the most effective method for illustrating the machine's usefulness. Under Patterson's watchful eye, the company's sales force drove relentlessly into new territory, imaginatively introducing the cash register to an endless number and variety of enterprises around the world. NCR cash registers appeared not only in saloons and grocery stores, but became an indispensable part of everyday business in barbershops, hotels, theaters, amusement parks, governmental offices and other operations. Cash registers were even used to ring out those found guilty and fined in a court of law in Minnesota, where their "customers" were instructed to pay the "gentleman with the large diamond" on their way out. Knowing the value of a testimony by a satisfied customer, Patterson made sure his photographers captured images of thousands of businesses—from Muskogee, Oklahoma to Johannesburg, South Africa.

Perhaps the most remarkable images in the NCR Archive, however, relate to Patterson's efforts to improve the world around him. Because of his unflagging zeal for reform, the NCR Photograph Department was kept constantly busy recording both the good and bad aspects of life in the city of Dayton in order to supply the images needed for his endless production of lectures and publications presented to business, social and civic organizations across the community. Patterson's involvement with nearly every aspect of urban reform, and his determination to advance the city as an important industrial and commercial center, meant few issues were left untouched by NCR photographers. As a result, Patterson and his photographic corps left behind a remarkable collection of images documenting life in Dayton between 1897 and 1922, the year of his death.

The images compliment the city, and they criticize the city. A high-angle view shows a progressive urban center with a skyline increasingly dominated by high-rise office buildings; a contrasting view of the Miami-Erie Canal, which bordered the business district on the east, shows a waterway in sad decline, its banks littered with refuse. Views of South Park highlight the NCR factory neighborhood's neatly maintained homes and tastefully landscaped yards, while contrasting views of children standing in a dirty, unsanitary street of the Kossuth Colony clearly condemn the unsavory living conditions found in the labor colony of the Barney and Smith Car Works. The grubby, inhospitable grounds of the Dayton Malleable Iron Works are in sharp contrast with the neatly planted grounds of the Davis Sewing Machine Company. Together, the many scenes of homes, factories, schools, parks, playgrounds, hospitals and social services leave us with indelible images of a city coming of age in turn-of-the-century America.

The 100,000 glass plate negatives in the NCR Archive are the legacy of a visionary who believed it was the responsibility of every citizen to contribute his talents to bettering the lives of others. Sometimes a saint, sometimes a sinner, irascible, demanding and unpredictable, he was also untiring in his efforts to improve the lives of his employees, his fellow Daytonians and his fellowman around the world. His optimism for the future is clearly shown in his following prediction for the twentieth century:

Now comes the twentieth century. For what will it be noted?

P H I L A N T H R O P Y !

In the twentieth century disease will be almost dead, strikes will be dead,

poverty will be dead, war will be dead, animosity will be dead.

But man will live. And for all there will be but one country,

and that country will be the whole earth; and for all there will be but one hope—

that hope the whole heaven.

A GROUP OF FOREIGN
COMMISSIONERS FROM
THE ST. LOUIS WORLD'S
FAIR STAND ON THE LAWN
OF THE NATIONAL CASH
REGISTER COMPANY,
SEPTEMBER 15, 1904.

THE PLATES

The following photographs are digitally scanned from the 100,000 glass plate
negatives contained in the NCR Archive. These large-format negatives are amazing for their clarity
and for the immense amount of information contained on the glass,
much of which is not even visible to the human eye without magnification.
The Archive in its entirely contains approximately 1.5 million images. The glass plate negative
is the earliest photographic format used by the NCR Photograph Department
and was used throughout the time period of John H. Patterson.
Although NCR began to use nitrate film about 1917, they continued to use the glass plate negatives.
In the following photos, the original labels have been retained;
the information below augments and illuminates the understanding of the reader.

DOWNTOWN

We progress through change. We must keep our eyes wide open

to rapid changes and improvements of the times.

We must expect them and keep in line of them. We must reflect how the world has changed

in the last 100 years and realize that it is now moving with tremendous rapidity.

Greater wonders will come to pass in the next decade than in the past ten centuries.

JOHN H. PATTERSON

Stand either upon the Dayton View bridge or the Main Street bridge, and look up or

down the river. Note the curving of the shores, the reflected foliage of the trees,

the symphony of colors blending with the browns and reds and grays. There you have a picture

more glorious than anything in the art galleries of Europe, more inspiring then anything

that was ever put upon the canvas by the hand of man.

DAYTON DAILY NEWS, 1915

By the turn of the twentieth century, Dayton had grown from a provincial small town to a bustling mid-sized city. After weathering the severe economic downturn of the 1890s, it emerged from its cocoon to take its place as a leader in progressivism among the nation's urban centers.

The downtown reflected this change. Tall office buildings and large department stores sprang up as developers raced to keep pace with the growing needs of business, government and retail. The commercial district reached outward from Main Street, encroaching on the neighborhoods of the city's wealthy, causing residents to cast their eyes toward the new green suburbs on the city's edge.

Despite these changes, much of the old nineteenth-century city continued to co-exist alongside the new. Modern skyscrapers dwarfed the small-scale Victorian commercial buildings of an earlier era, blocking from view the graceful church spires that had previously dominated the skyline. Downtown continued to be home to many of Dayton's wealthier citizens, although the 1913 flood would make the high ground of the suburbs more enticing.

Under the direction of John Patterson, NCR photographers carefully recorded downtown, capturing on glass a city at its zenith as a commercial and industrial center. The images of busy streets in a prosperous central business district surrounded by peaceful neighborhoods reflected Patterson's deep pride in the city of his birth. Always quick to set forth his opinions on what needed changing, however, he also documented some of the city's more negative features, such as the abandoned Miami-Erie Canal and the grade railroad crossings which congested traffic and exacted a terrible human toll. Using these images in countless publications and lectures, Patterson promoted, praised, and criticized his city, bringing about positive change in a community which became known nationwide for its energetic leadership and innovative civic ideals.

MAIN STREET BRIDGE, SEPTEMBER 2, 1910

By the early 1900s, the wood and iron bridges of an earlier era were giving way to modern bridges of steel and concrete construction. Although other bridge designs would have been more economical, Dayton's leaders opted for the more expensive concrete bridges, whose graceful arches, balustrades and decorative lamps lent an air of urban sophistication and European elegance to the city. The Main Street bridge was built in 1902–1903. In the background stands Steele High School.

MAIN AND THIRD

On a warm day sometime around 1910, an NCR photographer captured this peaceful downtown scene on Main Street looking north from just below Third. Notice that the automobiles are parked diagonally, a custom undoubtedly adapted from the age-old practice of parking a horse at a hitching post. This parking pattern would continue until October 30, 1942 when diagonal parking was prohibited on the city's main thoroughfares.

KRESGE'S FIVE AND TEN CENT STORE

This discount chain was established in 1897 in Detroit and Memphis by John G. McCrory and Sebastian S. Kresge, "a man so cheap he gave up golf because he couldn't stand to lose the balls." Kresge became sole owner in 1907, operating eight stores in cities from Pittsburgh to Chicago. At first, he kept the prices to not more than ten cents, but inflation brought on by World War I pushed it upward to fifteen cents. This photo of the Kresge store at 131 South Main Street was taken about 1910. Many years later, Kresge would become the well-known Kmart discount chain store.

WILKIE'S NEWSSTAND AT THIRD AND MAIN, MAY 20, 1913

Wilkie's News was established in 1894 by Julius Wilkie. With the rapid growth in the number and popularity of newspapers and magazines in the late nineteenth century, newsstands became indispensable sources for news and other information. The location at the busy intersection at Third and Main provided a steady stream of customers for Wilkie, who used the cart as a temporary measure after the 1913 flood destroyed his store at 32 West Fifth Street.

TRACTION CAR, THIRD AND JEFFERSON, 1910

This downtown street scene focuses on an interurban car of the Ohio Electric Railway Company, which controlled 600 miles of electric road and connected many of the principal cities in Ohio and Indiana. At one end, freight is being loaded for shipment, while on the other passengers crowd on board for rapid transport, perhaps to Columbus. By 1910, Dayton was one of the leading traction centers in the nation. Although the interurban system was a fast and efficient mode of transportation, it would soon be replaced by the automobile, which allowed Americans to travel anywhere on a whim without the need to conform to a public schedule.

DAYTON PUBLIC LIBRARY, COOPER PARK, OCTOBER 29, 1911

The growth of the nation's cities in the years after the Civil War was accompanied by an increased emphasis on education and the development of public library systems. Dayton, like many communities, struggled to expand its library collections and services to meet the demands placed on it by a growing population and the expansion of its high-precision industries. In 1884, leading Dayton citizens secured permission from City Council to build in Cooper Park and selected the local architectural firm of Peters & Burns to design the new library. The imposing Romanesque style building, constructed of Dayton limestone with red sandstone trim, was dedicated January 24, 1888.

COUNTY JAIL, MAY 12, 1913

The county jail and sheriff's office was built in 1874 on West Third Street, at the rear of the Old Court House. In 1909, the Reverend A. W. Drury, Dayton citizen and historian, stated that the jail and the 1884 courthouse (located where courthouse square is today) were "the first public buildings making the change from an irregular, half-conscious town to an awakened city of solid character and teeming life." While this might have been overstated (the 1850 Old Court House is still considered one of the finest buildings erected in America in the nineteenth century), the substantial Second Empire style jail certainly contributed greatly to the increasing architectural sophistication of the downtown streetscape.

ROTARY CLUB ON MAIN STREET MARCHING TO BRIDGE, CIRCA 1910

      This view, looking south from Steele High School at Main and Monument, shows a parade with Rotarians in the lead moving towards the Main Street bridge. The first Rotary Club was formed in Chicago in 1905 to promote fellowship among the business community. The name "Rotary" came from the practice of rotating the meetings between the offices of the various members.

      In the background is the Victoria Theater; the block between the theater and the school would later be the site of the Biltmore Hotel. At center is an Overland car dealership. Overland, one of many car manufacturers which appeared in the early twentieth century, became the Willys-Overland Motor Company in 1908; from 1912 to 1918 the company was second in sales only to the Ford Motor Company.

THE PHILLIPS HOUSE, 1913 FLOOD

After the floodwaters receded, Daytonians lost no time in cleaning up and getting back to business as usual. Here, street crews work to clear away layers of the foul-smelling mud coating city streets. This photograph, showing the rapid restoration of downtown, was taken from behind the Old Court House, looking southeast towards the corner of Third and Main. The Phillips House is at center; the Conover Building (now the RTA Transit Pavilion) is the tall office building towards the left side of the photograph.

POPCORN AND PEANUT STAND AT COURTHOUSE

For many years this peanut and popcorn stand was a familiar sight at its location beside the Old Court House at Third and Main Streets. Little is known about its history, although it is said to have been owned and operated by "Sam, the Spanish-American War veteran." This photograph was taken about 1912 to document the installation of a new NCR Class 300 cash register.

VICTORIA THEATER, MAIN AND FIRST, SEPTEMBER 1913

The Victoria Theater, built as Turner's Opera House by West Carrollton brewers William and Joseph Turner, opened January 1, 1866. On May 16, 1869 it burned in one of Dayton's most disastrous fires, which also destroyed several surrounding buildings. Rebuilt in 1871 as Music Hall, by 1885 it had become known as the Grand Opera House. It later became the Victoria Opera House, and was renamed the Victoria Theater in 1901. Although the scene of many refined musical and theatrical performances, it seemed (at least on the exterior) to lack some of the elegance it has today. In addition to being a center for the arts, it housed a plumbing service, an Oldsmobile and Oakland office, and a paint and wallpaper store. At top, large signs advertised the Goodrich Tire Company and The Green & Green Company, ornaments now unthinkable for this stately performance hall.

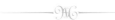

CONVENTION STAGE AND AUDIENCE IN GRAND OPERA HOUSE, OCTOBER 1896

John Patterson early on mastered the art of using conventions as tools to motivate, educate, and reward employees. In October 1896, he chose to hold his week-long international sales convention at the Grand Opera House (now the Victoria Theater), whose beautifully appointed interior provided an appropriate backdrop for his elaborately staged production. Prizes were awarded to factory workers for the best suggestions, to foremen for the best improvements in departmental operations, and to sales agents for outstanding selling performances. Patterson also used the opportunity to showcase his newly completed manufacturing complex, already declared to be "the model factory of the world," to the hundreds of outside manufacturers and merchants who were invited to attend the convention and tour the factory.

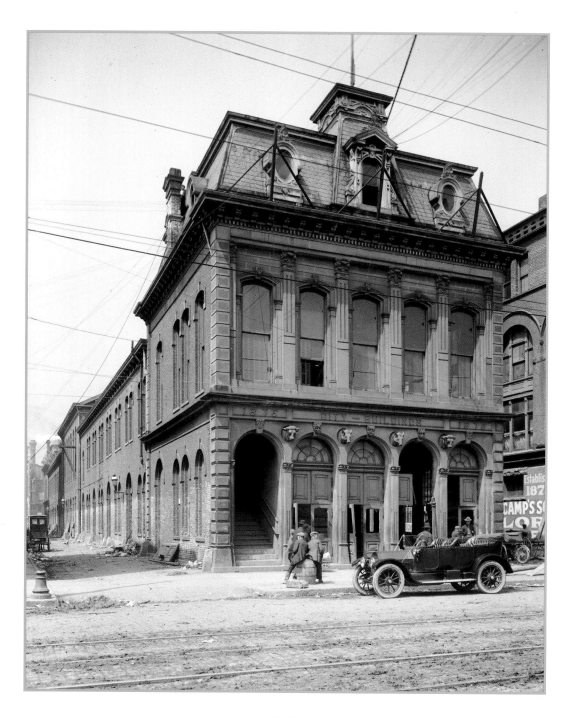

CITY BUILDING, MAY 6, 1913

This photograph shows the City Building and Market House a little the worse for wear after the disastrous flood which occurred just six weeks earlier. The entrance doors, badly warped by the flood waters, hang ajar, and the side street is littered with debris still waiting to be removed by municipal clean-up crews. Unmindful of the clutter, two men take a break on an improvised seat on the sidewalk's edge, while on the second story city business continues as usual. This Second Empire style building was located on the east side of South Main between Third and Fourth Streets, and was built in 1876.

MAIN STREET MARKET, OCTOBER 1917

This photograph offers a close-up view of a downtown market day in the fall of 1917. Women with baskets inspect produce and barter for prices, while a few enterprising merchants, such as the man wearing the "Postum" placard, take the opportunity to sell the public on their wares. Taken on an overcast or foggy day, this photo may illustrate the smoke problem, a growing concern in large urban centers by the turn of the century. In 1907, Dayton reformers attempted to push through a smoke abatement ordinance requiring factories, locomotives, hotels, schools, apartment buildings and other large buildings to install smoke consumers. NCR and twenty-one other manufacturers joined together to oppose the ordinance, claiming that it would result in a stoppage of business and that effective smoke consumers were not yet available.

J. B. HEISS FLOWER STORE, MARCH 23, 1904

This floral shop, located at 112 South Main Street, was the retail outlet of J. B. Heiss, who owned The Exotic Nurseries and Greenhouses at the northeast corner of East Fifth and Findlay Streets. A landscape gardener, he specialized in palms which, by the turn of the century, had become a favorite decorative device in homes and businesses. Heiss was an internationally known businessman, who by 1904 controlled the palm trade in the area between New York, Chicago and New Orleans.

NORTH MAIN AND SHILOH BUS

This photograph shows a jitney (a small bus) standing outside the Dayton Daily News building at Ludlow and Fourth Streets. Jitneys may have been used to extend the reach of Dayton's transportation services as the city spread far beyond the reach of the streetcar lines. The introduction of the diesel motor bus would eventually bring about the demise of the railed streetcar system.

JEFFERSON STREET LOOKING SOUTH FROM POINT NORTH OF THIRD,
JULY 28, 1904

By 1900, the downtown streetscape was characterized by a remarkable tangle of overhead wires, the result of the multiple streetcar and interurban companies servicing the city. This photograph, which appeared in an NCR civic reform publication in 1904, was taken to illustrate the "menace" presented by the profusion of wires downtown. The trolley wire issue continued to spark debate throughout the period, despite reformers' attempts to bring about the consolidation of streetcar lines and to reduce the number of wires crisscrossing the city.

LAND BETWEEN COOPER PARK AND CANAL, NORTH OF THIRD STREET

This photo shows the muddy, nearly impassable road running along the west side of the derelict Miami-Erie Canal. The canal was a particular complaint of John Patterson's, who decried the wasteful amount of public funds being put into rejuvenating what he saw as a long outdated mode of transportation. To make matters worse, the unsightly road and waterway ran alongside Cooper Park (at left), the city's oldest green space and the location of the modern and beautiful public library. Patterson would eventually get his way; in the 1920s the canal would be filled in and the roadway named "Patterson Boulevard" in his honor. Patterson Boulevard opened to traffic in 1939.

REIBOLD BUILDING, SEPTEMBER 2, 1910

The ten-story Reibold Building, designed by Dayton architect Charles Insco Williams, was built in 1896 and was the city's second skyscraper. Williams designed many Dayton buildings in this period, including Stivers High School, the Algonquin Hotel, Newcom Manor, Sacred Heart Church, and the Callahan Bank Building. The annex (the plainer section on the left) was constructed in 1904.

ELDER AND JOHNSTON'S, STORE EXTERIOR

The Elder and Johnston dry goods company began business on East Third Street in 1883, and moved to the Reibold Building on South Main just south of Fourth Street in 1896. Previously the city's dry goods stores were centered on Third between Main and Jefferson Streets, and were small establishments whose limited stock frustrated shoppers. By the 1890s, however, the era of the large department store was in full swing, and spacious multi-floor stores offering a wide variety of goods formed the new Main Street shopping district. At the turn of the century, the most fashionable shopping area was around Fourth and Main, where all the more substantial stores (including Rike's, Traxler's and Oelman's) were located. Elder and Johnston's was the largest of these operations, employing 350 persons in twenty-six departments.

MAIN STREET RAILROAD CROSSING BLOCKED BY TRAIN,
NOVEMBER 10, 1917

The city's heavy rail traffic not only created endless delays, but also killed and maimed large numbers of adults and children who tried unsuccessfully to navigate the dangerous grade crossings. Daytonians hotly debated the issue of grade crossings for over fifty years, at one time slowing trains to a crawl, which increased congestion and enticed boys to try the sometimes deadly sport of jumping onto moving railroad cars. By 1918, steam railroads were carrying more than two million passengers a year in and out of the city, and the proliferation of automobiles only added to the traffic snarl caused by slow-moving trains.

LOWE BROTHERS PAINT STORE

The Lowe Brothers Paint Store was located on the southeast corner of Third and Jefferson Streets. The company began in 1872 when Henry C. Lowe and Houston Lowe formed the firm of Lowe Brothers, dealers in paint, varnish, oil, glass and painters' supplies. In 1883, they began to manufacture paint, gradually building a reputation for both a high-quality product and for their progressive business methods. The Lowe Brothers Company was incorporated in 1893. In 1897, the Lowes decided to confine their efforts solely to manufacturing and sold the store to Horace A. Irvin, secretary of The Lowe Brothers Company.

U. B. BUILDING

For many years Dayton was the home of the United Brethren Publishing House, one of the most important publishing houses in the nation. Its tall office building at the northeast corner of Fourth and Main was the vision of William R. Funk, who was elected publishing agent in 1897. According to Publishing House board member Dr. A. W. Drury, Funk "always stood for a progressive policy, so much so that he managed to have the church and the board half-scared a good part of the time." Believing modern business methods could be used to improve man's condition, Funk dreamed of building an office tower whose profits would provide adequate pensions for retired ministers and their families. Completed in 1905, the building was designed by Dayton architect Charles Herby, and was built by the F. A. Requarth Company. Situated on prime real estate land in the central business district, the office building provided a high profile for what was for many years the city's leading Protestant denomination. The United Brethren sold the building in 1952; today it is known as the Centre City Building.

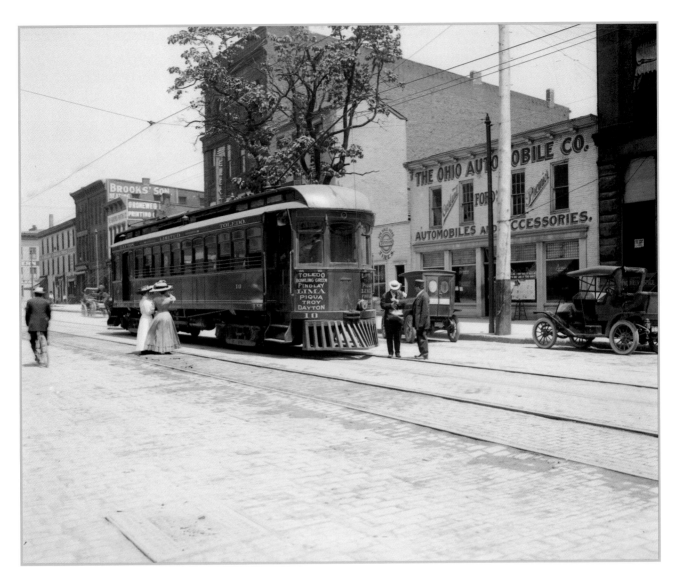

DAYTON TOLEDO TRACTION CAR ON NORTH JEFFERSON STREET

At the turn of the century, Dayton enjoyed a reputation as one of the leading traction centers in the nation. The city's first interurban line was the Cincinnati and Dayton which began operation in 1895. By 1907 the city's traction lines were carrying 300,000 passengers per month; in 1919 they provided service to more than four million passengers. Fast and convenient, many thought the interurbans would revolutionize both passenger and freight service. Unfortunately, within a few decades the coming of the automobile and the motor bus derailed the promise of the traction lines, making them a short-lived transportation phenomenon. Ironically, although this photograph focuses on the traction car, the new mode of transportation is very evident in the automobiles parked in front of the Ohio Automobile Company, a dealer in automobiles and accessories.

FORUM BAR, NOVEMBER 7, 1913

Dayton's many bars were important social centers for the city's working class, and, until the 1890s, were one of the few places a man could go for a meal served outside the home. Many of these saloons featured garish, but picturesque, interiors with ceramic tile floors, carved ladies, gilded mirrors and ornate tin ceilings. For years, urban reformers had pointed to the saloon as the root of all urban evils, and in 1895 the Anti-Saloon League was founded, which led the campaign for prohibition. Although John Patterson's earliest sales were primarily made to the saloon trade, he himself was a teetotaler who abhorred the effect of drink on employees' health and efficiency. Despite his own aversion to alcohol, however, saloons continued to be important NCR customers. Here, employees and clientele of the Forum Bar pose for a company photographer. The Forum was located on the east side of Main between Fifth and Sixth Streets.

FIFTH AND LUDLOW STREETS, SOUTHWEST CORNER, CIRCA 1911

When this photograph was taken, South Ludlow Street was still a quiet residential neighborhood located away from the bustle of the central business district. This corner building features a fascinating combination of businesses, including a cigar shop and shine parlor; a Chinese laundry and Japanese bazaar; and a photographer's studio. By the turn of the century, advances in technology had made it possible to offer a wide range of photographic services. This photographer used the building as a billboard, advertising photographs ("16 for 25 cents"), postcards ("made while you wait"), and night photography. Attached on the right is an early curbside fast food restaurant. While this scene might seem charming to us, the billboard exterior of the building was probably photographed as an "unsightly place in Dayton," the category Patterson assigned to sites that detracted from the cityscape and were to be targets for urban reform.

VIEW FROM ROOF OF ALGONQUIN HOTEL LOOKING NORTH

This photograph was taken about 1900 from the roof of the Algonquin Hotel at the corner of Third and Ludlow. During this period, Dayton was frequently referred to as the "city of churches" (as was Brooklyn, New York), and certainly the graceful spires were still a prominent part of the city skyline. This idyllic scene shows a quiet, tree-lined neighborhood filled with the large and stylish homes of Dayton's wealthy who, in the era before the automobile, preferred to live within easy walking distance of church, school and work. Skyscrapers were beginning to transform the Dayton skyline, but the few standing at this time were just to the right of the photographer's range, giving us a more nineteenth-century view of the city.

TURNING THE OAKWOOD CAR AROUND, TAKEN AT THE DAYTON VIEW BRIDGE

In 1907, Daytonians narrowly averted the collapse of the Dayton View bridge which had not been designed to handle the heavy streetcar and automobile traffic of the twentieth century. According to the Dayton Journal's June 1st account, Mr. Estabrook and Mr. Horn were driving on the bridge and met an Oakwood streetcar going the opposite direction. Mr. Estabrook noticed "a peculiar swing in the middle span of the bridge" and upon inspection discovered that the span was giving way. Traffic was immediately stopped and the bridge closed. The closure necessitated the manual turning of the Oakwood streetcar when it reached the temporary end of its route at the Dayton View bridge. The old iron structure was replaced by a modern concrete bridge in 1909–1910.

RIKE'S DRY GOODS HOUSE, FOURTH AND MAIN STREETS

In 1893, the Rike Dry Goods Company moved from its small store on Third Street to this monumental building with square tower and graceful dome on the southwest corner of Fourth and Main. Built before the days of ready-made garments, David Rike set out to mitigate the challenges of his women shoppers by offering mezzanine space to many of the city's best dressmakers. Customers could first visit the dressmaker to select a pattern and then conveniently purchase the fabric and trimmings on the main floor without ever having to leave the building.

This store was built without sidewalk display windows. Frederick Rike eventually convinced his father to add the windows, but only on the condition that they would be covered with shades on Sundays. There was to be no shopping—not even window shopping—on the Lord's Day!

FRONT OF RIKE-KUMLER, DECEMBER 9, 1913

The Rike-Kumler Company relocated to its new building at Second and Main in 1912, despite the negative comments of skeptics who wondered why any astute businessman would move his business so far from the city's premier shopping district at Fourth and Main. The ladies lost no time in patronizing this large and well-stocked department store, where they could easily pass an entire day shopping with friends.

On a sunny day two weeks before Christmas, an NCR photographer captured this scene taken at the Main Street entrance of the new store, which had made a remarkable recovery after the 1913 flood. At left, two women inspect the lacy neckwear tastefully displayed in the large plate glass windows, while at right a member of the Salvation Army, which had begun operating in the city in the 1890s, solicits donations to fund Christmas dinners for needy Daytonians.

ATLAS HOTEL AND NEW YMCA BUILDING, CIRCA 1907

This photograph documents the construction of the YMCA building erected in 1907–1908 on the northwest corner of Third and Ludlow Streets. Designed by the Dayton architectural firm of Peters, Burns and Pretzinger, it was built of concrete made by the Ferro Construction Company of Cincinnati, said to be the foremost concrete construction concern in the world. The Journal declared the new building to be the largest and most complete YMCA in the nation. The cornerstone was laid by Secretary of War William Howard Taft on April 28, 1907. It was a fitting tribute to Taft's father, Alphonso, who came with a group of men from Cincinnati in 1857 to encourage the organization of a YMCA in Dayton. After the present building was constructed on Monument Avenue in 1929, this "Y" became an office building. It was sold to the City of Dayton in 1940 and is now City Hall. At right is the Atlas Hotel built in 1893.

UNION STATION, DAYTON, OHIO

     According to Dayton chronicler Charlotte Reeve Conover, "no improvement really changed the appearance of the city like the new union railway station completed in January 1901." The station was built despite conflicts among the numerous railway companies operating in the city and citizen concerns over the future elevation of the tracks. The classically styled Union Station with patterned brick façade and square clock tower was built during a period when it was a point of pride for cities to build large and architecturally imposing railway stations as doorways to the community. In 1907, the Dayton Journal boasted that the city had the finest Union Railroad Station in Ohio, and handled 110 trains daily.

CONSTRUCTION OF BUILDING CORNER FOURTH AND LUDLOW SHOWING
STREET BLOCKED WITH LUMBER LYING AROUND SIDEWALK, APRIL 3, 1907

The above label reflects Patterson's irritation over the public hazard posed by the messy construction site, blocking not only the sidewalk, but also half of Ludlow Street. The building in progress was the ten-story Commercial Building, designed by Albert Pretzinger, and one of many downtown buildings erected by the Schantz family in the early twentieth century. Daytonians were proud of the many new buildings in the central business district, and boasted that "the Commercial will take its place in the constellation of pretty, large and modern office buildings that is marking the material progress of the city." At left is the Algonquin Hotel, completed in 1899 and expanded in 1904. The "fire proof" sign at the top of this steel and concrete building documents a growing preoccupation with fire prevention, which began in earnest after a particularly destructive fire in Baltimore in 1904.

SACRED HEART CHURCH, CORNER FOURTH AND WILKINSON STREETS, SEPTEMBER 3, 1910

The Church of the Sacred Heart was established in 1883. The exterior of the Romanesque style church, built of Dayton limestone with Berea brownstone trim, was completed in 1889. The building was dedicated November 10, 1895. It was designed by Dayton architect, Charles Insco Williams, whose work can still be seen throughout downtown. Today, we think of this stately Roman Catholic church as being located in the midst of the central business district, but as the photo shows, it was originally nestled in the midst of a peaceful, tree-lined neighborhood, within easy walking distance of its many parishioners.

CONOVER BUILDING

The thirteen-story building at the southeast corner of Third and Main was erected in 1900 by the Conover Building Company. It was designed by Frank Andrews, the architect who also designed NCR's famed sunlight factory buildings and the Third Street Arcade. Andrews later became nationally known for his work in hotel design, and was also the architect for the Kentucky state capitol. The Conover Building, the city's third skyscraper, dwarfed the adjacent low-lying Victorian business blocks of the nineteenth century.

BUILDING THE LIBERTY LOAN CASH REGISTER, 1918

Advertising, a sales method which grew exponentially in the early years of the twentieth century, was used very effectively during World War I to promote American unity and support for the war effort. Daytonians built this giant cash register in 1918 on the lawn of the Old Court House at Third and Main to encourage contributions to the Fourth Liberty Loan campaign. Used to indicate the daily total subscriptions, it was at the time the largest cash register ever built. The Old Court House, completed in 1850, has been the scene of many of the community's most important rallies and celebrations.

MIAMI HOTEL, NORTHEAST CORNER SECOND AND LUDLOW

Many believed that the 1913 flood spelled the end of the city's prosperity, predicting that it would take ten years to clear away the mounds of debris. Daytonians completed clean-up in a mere ten weeks, but public opinion still held that Dayton would never make a comeback. To silence skeptics, one hundred Dayton businessmen, led by John Patterson, banded together to erect the million-dollar Miami Hotel. The elegant, richly furnished hotel, said to be "positively the last word in all that the modern hotel affords," featured all the amenities including air conditioning and piped-in ice water in each room. The hotel opened Saturday, October 9, 1915 with a grand celebration. It provided lodging to many of the nation's rich and famous, including William Howard Taft, Henry Ford and Jack Dempsey.

TAXIS AND OTHER CONVEYANCES USED DURING STREETCAR STRIKE, 1920

Sunday morning of June 20, 1920 found Daytonians walking to church, as the city faced the third street railway strike in three years. The sixteen-day strike involved the 600 motormen of the City, Peoples' and Dayton Street railways, all members of the Amalgamated Association of Street and Electric Railway Employees of America. Over 400 automobile owners, seeing a way to make a profit, paid the city $1.00 for a permit to transform their private autos into taxis, and thirty buses were brought from Toledo to ease the hardship caused by the sudden lack of streetcar service. The strike greatly increased downtown congestion, trying the patience of city police. Officer George Saunders, stationed at the city's busiest intersection at Third and Main stated, "Automobiles going by my corner have doubled in number since the strike. And then in addition to them, I have to give the 'Stop' and 'Go' signs to many other conveyances not used before, such as junk wagons, bicycles, ancient cabs and hacks and even roller skates."

"SAFETY FIRST" SIGN, THIRD AND MAIN, CIRCA 1920

The growth of cities was accompanied by a corresponding increase in traffic problems, which were largely attributed to the explosion in the number of automobiles in the first two decades of the twentieth century. The slogan "safety first" appeared everywhere, even on this downtown street sign reminding pedestrians of the elementary rule to look both ways before crossing the street. Dayton conducted at least one "Safety Week" campaign in this period, in order to teach both youth and adults to take appropriate safety precautions. America had more accidents than any other two or three countries in the world combined; in 1922 alone 14,000 Americans died in motor accidents. Sixty-seven percent of these fatalities were due to the automobile, more than four times the number caused by trains and seven times the number due to streetcar accidents. Even as early as 1920, the high-accident rate was attributed to the American pattern of hurry and rush, which made Americans much more accident prone than those living in slower-paced countries in other parts of the world.

DAYTON AUTO SHOW, MEMORIAL HALL, CIRCA 1912

In the early years of the twentieth century, many Ohio cities built grand halls to honor their communities' veterans. In 1906, Montgomery County citizens voted for a $250,000 bond to erect a Memorial Building at the corner of St. Clair and First Streets. By January 1907, the Memorial Building trustees had accepted the plans prepared by architect W. E. Russ and had selected noted Dayton architect Albert Pretzinger as consulting architect.

Dedicated January 5, 1910, the Beaux Arts style building featured a grand memorial hall complete with Tiffany windows and an auditorium with a seating capacity of 3,500. The latter was designed with a flat floor to accommodate a wide range of activities from boxing matches to orchestra performances. The signage changed to fit the culture of the event: "No spitting" signs were posted for the more demonstrative crowds attending the boxing matches, but were covered over for the politely restrained symphony audiences.

This image shows the Dayton Auto Show held at Memorial Hall around 1912, which exhibited the latest products from Cadillac and other automobile companies. The stylish Japanese décor with delicate dogwoods and paper lanterns increased the air of class and sophistication surrounding the event.

TRAXLER'S DEPARTMENT STORE, CIRCA 1918

World War I touched every aspect of life in Dayton, even its advertising. The war greatly changed life in the Gem City, which at one point was second in the nation in war production. Dayton began its first munitions work in 1915 with the receipt of an $80 million contract from the Russian government. After the United States entered the war, government contracts poured in, causing many Dayton plants to completely reorganize operations to handle wartime needs. In 1916, at least $30 million of munitions were manufactured in Dayton, and by 1918 at least 12,000 persons were employed in munitions work in the city.

M c C O O K   F I E L D

McCook Field was established during World War I as a military aviation research center. Many nationally known engineers and skilled mechanics were brought to the air field to advance aeronautics for national defense. The field was limited by its small size, and for Dayton to retain its position as the national center of aeronautical research it had to develop larger facilities. As a result, the experimental work being conducted at McCook was eventually transferred to Wright Field.

the NEIGHBORHOODS

A city is a great enterprise whose stockholders are the people.

JOHN H. PATTERSON

There are those who object to the breaking up of a city into sections—

into a North Dayton, and East Dayton, and West Dayton, and Riverdale, and Dayton View,

These people claim that it ought not to be done, for the reason

⟨re all in Dayton; but there is another way of looking at it.

⟨le friendly rivalries we promote a sort of jealousy that is crystallized

⟨lowers about the homes, in better living conditions,

⟨happier children, and in a higher grade citizenship.

ON DAILY NEWS, JUNE 12, 1915

```
       BOOKS  &  CO.
05/02    09:06    H    13      6793
1@ 25.00 0972096507  10%$     22.50
          DAYTON COMES OF
TOTAL        9011645418  $    22.50
ES TAX @ 6.500%          $     1.46
AL                       $    23.96
DER Cash                 $    23.96

r Savings!               $     2.50


ICHOLAS P. MONEY DISCUSSES HIS BOOK,
  BLOOMFIELD'S ORCHARD', 10/5, 2-3 PM
```

⟨ntury a growing population and changing ideas on the appropriate place to raise a family meant that more and more Daytonians chose to make their homes in the suburbs outside the city center. Suburban living had begun as early as the 1830s with development of the Oregon neighborhood, and continued to expand throughout the nineteenth century, bringing the establishment of neighborhoods such as South Park, Riverdale and West Dayton. The electrification of streetcar lines in 1888 and the coming of the automobile in the early twentieth century (coupled with the 1913 flood which made Daytonians think twice about living in low lying areas) greatly accelerated the move to new suburbs such as Oakwood and Dayton View.

These years brought a nationwide emphasis on the role of a proper home environment in the nurturing of the child and in the preservation of democracy. Urban reformers fought vigorously for the development of parks and recreation centers, and encouraged the development of neighborhoods with beautifully landscaped lawns and wide open spaces.

John Patterson, the city's most vocal and colorful exponent of these new ideas, began his campaign for reform in the factory neighborhood of South Park which, when NCR moved from downtown to Brown Street in the 1880s, was a less than reputable neighborhood known by the unflattering name of Slidertown. In the mid-1890s he called the residents together, announced the name change to South Park, and began an energetic reform program that in three years transformed one of the seamier sides of Dayton into one of its most attractive neighborhoods. Through illustrated lectures, he proceeded to spread his ideas throughout Dayton, making the city known as one of the best landscaped in America. The neighborhood images focus on parks, landscaping and other improvements, as well as showing areas in need of social reform. They also include photographs taken to document cash register sales to local merchants, which allow us to catch a glimpse of the many long-vanished businesses located on streetcar lines and on corners throughout the city's neighborhoods.

ALEX SPATZ GROCERY, 1921

Before the automobile and other innovations ushered in the era of the large grocery chain, urban dwellers depended on the "mom-and-pop" stores located on neighborhood corners and along streetcar routes throughout the city. The Alex S. Spatz grocery at 1925 North Main Street was just one of over 400 small operations listed in the city directory in 1921. Here, Mr. Spatz and family pose for an NCR photographer, who was documenting yet another purchase of a National cash register.

EAST THIRD STREET LOOKING EAST AT SPRINGFIELD STREET

This peaceful East Dayton street scene shows several types of businesses long since vanished from our urban landscape, including a feed store, a coal yard and an express freight depot. A closer look reveals a near miss of an interurban car with a horse and wagon, illustrating the potential for disaster when slower moving vehicles failed to yield the right-of-way to the faster moving street and traction cars. The newspapers regularly reported accidents, such as the 1913 collision between an Ohio Electric traction car and a horse-drawn wagon, which killed George Federer, a driver for the Olt Brewery Company, and his team of horses. His partner escaped by bailing out of the wagon before impact.

LANDSCAPE GARDENING, JUDGING LAWNS ON KIEFABER STREET

Like many urban reformers of the 1890s, John Patterson believed that the home should be a clean, comfortable refuge surrounded by artistically landscaped yards, creating a restful, park-like atmosphere appropriate for the raising of children. To encourage neighborhood improvement, Patterson offered instruction in landscaping, provided free seeds and plantings, and gave generous prizes for the best landscaped yards. This photo shows judges for the annual competition in the South Park neighborhood inspecting the landscaping at 452 Kiefaber Street. Patterson's methods were successful; the famed Olmsted Brothers, the landscaping firm which designed New York's Central Park and the NCR factory grounds, declared Park Avenue in South Park to be "the most beautiful street of its class in America."

CHILDREN IN THE KOSSUTH COLONY, MAY 8, 1919

The Kossuth Colony was established in August 1905 by Jacob Moskowitz to provide laborers for the Barney & Smith Car Works, one of the foremost manufacturers of railroad cars in the country. By 1906, Moskowitz built about forty houses just outside of the city limits on a twelve-acre tract of land east of Troy and north of Leo Streets. The majority of its residents were Hungarians (500–600), but there were also about 100 Rumanians and a few members of other nationalities. The twelve-foot fence surrounding the colony quickly set off a city-wide controversy. Moskowitz claimed that he was protecting non-English speaking immigrants from being victimized by foreign labor agents and other outsiders, while many Daytonians believed he had the less honorable intention of controlling the lives and pocketbooks of Kossuth residents. The colony was short lived; the 1913 flood brought on the gradual demise of the great car works which had given birth to the colony, and by 1921 Kossuth had passed into private hands. This photograph used children to emphasize the ill-effects of the colony's dirty streets and shabby housing.

WAYNE AVENUE MARKET HOUSE RECONSTRUCTION, JUNE 1913

The Market House, located at Wayne and Burns Avenues (now covered over by U.S. 35), was one of two market buildings owned by the City of Dayton. Left dirty and unfit for public use by the 1913 flood, the market nevertheless continued to operate until officials closed it as a public health hazard on May 24th. Unable to secure cooperation from the city in cleaning up the market, an appeal was finally made to John Patterson, who responded by sending a team of one hundred workers from NCR equipped with mops, buckets, lumber and other tools to remedy the situation. Twenty-eight hours later the market was completely cleaned and sanitized; workers had even managed to give the walls a fresh coat of paint. The Wayne Avenue Market reopened on June 4th, as Patterson promised, to the strains of a band specially provided by the company for the grand event.

CORNER SECOND AND MONTGOMERY STREETS, MARCH 22, 1912

On a chilly spring day three ladies pose on the porch of a house in Dayton's eastern industrial district. Although known for the landscaped beauty of its neighborhoods, some of the city's residents still lived in less than desirable circumstances. This unkempt house with its barren, debris-littered yard was undoubtedly photographed to illustrate the continuing need for reform. Despite the "furnished rooms for rent" sign, the city was experiencing a housing shortage, most critical for the growing number of women coming to work in the city's thriving industries. Frequently landlords were unwilling to rent to women, increasing the urgency for the development of housing by the YWCA and other social agencies.

DAKOTA AND CHADWICK STREETS, APRIL 4, 1912

In 1898, the Dayton Malleable Iron Company hired Jacob Moskowitz, a Hungarian Jew, to bring Eastern Europeans to the city to labor in the iron works. Moskowitz recruited workers from east coast cities, settling them in the West Side Colony, a small area bounded by Broadway, West Third Street, Negley Place, and Summit Street (now Paul Laurence Dunbar Street), which was conveniently located adjacent to Dayton Malleable. The colony contained about 6,000 immigrants, including large numbers of Hungarians and Rumanians, and smaller numbers of Poles, Greeks, Macedonians, Serbs, Croatians, Bulgarians, Turks and Russians. Unlike Kossuth, the labor colony located in North Dayton, the West Side Colony was not walled and residents were free to come and go as they pleased.

Here, children pose in front of a row of two-story gabled houses with unique chimney design. The photo was taken to show the undesirable living conditions found in the colony.

BAXTER STREET NORTH OF THE RAILROAD

This photograph of Baxter Street on Dayton's West Side was probably taken to document recently completed improvements; indeed, the new sidewalks and fire hydrants shown here may have been the first modern city amenities to be introduced into the area. Baxter Street was renamed Dunbar Avenue in 1909, three years after the death of poet Paul Laurence Dunbar, and was home to many of Dayton's African American citizens. It was a small roadway, connecting West Fifth and Germantown Streets (and should not be confused with the present Paul Laurence Dunbar Street). The Holloway Children's Home, an orphanage privately operated by African American widow Julia Holloway, and numerous other black organizations were located there. The *History of the City of Dayton and Montgomery County, Ohio* also cited the construction of a new industrial plant about 1909 on Dunbar Avenue by Cyrus Baldwin, who owned much of the property on the street and who offered to sell the factory to black residents.

LANDSCAPE GARDENING, OXFORD AVENUE, NORTH SIDE
LOOKING WEST FROM BROADWAY, SEPTEMBER 1910

By the turn of the century many of Dayton's prominent citizens had left behind their grand old homes in the center city and moved to the new suburb of Dayton View. The neighborhood was carefully planned; setbacks were required allowing for generous front yards and fences were prohibited. John Patterson's city-wide lectures on landscaping had had their desired effect, imparting a park-like appearance to many neighborhoods and giving Dayton a reputation as one of the best landscaped cities in the nation. Here, an NCR photographer records the attractive yards and the row of young trees which would grow to provide shade for future generations.

WALNUT HILLS IMPROVEMENT ASSOCIATION
GUNCKEL AVENUE AND MARGARET STREET, SEPTEMBER 1913

The Walnut Hills Improvement Association was one of many citizens' organizations established in this period to encourage neighborhood beautification through careful planning and landscaping. This photograph shows a newly planted green space, with small trees and sparsely growing grass. Still in the early stages of development, many lots are vacant and streets are unpaved. The small frame church in the background is the Colorado Avenue Baptist Church. Walnut Hills became particularly popular after the flood in March of 1913 made suburban life on high ground seem like a great idea to many who lost homes and belongings in the turbulent waters.

BISHOP WRIGHT ON HIS PORCH AT 7 HAWTHORN

Bishop Milton Wright, the father of pioneer aviators Wilbur and Orville, noted in his diary the visit of an NCR photographer to the family home on Hawthorn Street on September 4, 1913. "Mr. Hardesty, of NCR...comes in an Automobile, with a photographer, and has him take pictures of Bigger's house and of ours including me, etc. I sat on the porch all forenoon; it was pleasant. Hardesty acts in behalf of Welfare department, NCR."

FRANK HALE'S GROCERY, CIRCA 1920

Hale's Liberty Market was located on the West Side on the southeast corner of Third and Williams Streets. It was one of dozens of small groceries scattered throughout the city's neighborhoods. This one was conveniently situated along the streetcar line, where it was easily accessible to neighborhood residents. Besides being a small business owner, Frank Hale took a leadership role in civic affairs, becoming mayor of Dayton in the early 1920s.

MOSELY COMMISSION VISITORS IN CARRIAGES ON WEST FIRST STREET, NOVEMBER 20, 1902

In the fall of 1902, Englishman Alfred Mosely and his committee of twenty-four craftsmen, who were in the United States investigating the conditions of American prosperity, stopped in Dayton to visit the NCR factory. Met by company carriages at Union Station, the visitors were treated to a grand tour of the downtown neighborhoods before heading out to Brown Street to see "the model factory of the world." They could not have failed to have been impressed by the wide streets and stately homes of the city's wealthy, many of whom still made their homes in this quiet residential neighborhood just west of the central business district.

VIEW OF LEVEE LOOKING EAST FROM MAIN, SEPTEMBER 11, 1912

   Before the height of the levees was raised as part of the Miami Conservancy District flood control plan, the levees were pleasant, shaded walkways frequented by residents who strolled their length enjoying the cool breezes and tranquil river scenery. Until the development of parks and recreation areas in the early years of the twentieth century, the levees were one of the few places Daytonians could go to escape the noise and congestion of city life.

BERTHA SCHMIDT GARDEN, 826 CINCINNATI STREET, JULY 5, 1912

This photograph was taken to show the Edgemont garden of Bertha Schmidt. The neighborhood was established in 1853 by John Patterson Brown and was originally known as "Patterson" or "Brownton." On John H. Patterson's suggestion, it was renamed "Edgemont" by residents who wanted a more suitable name for the rapidly growing suburb. The home of St. Elizabeth Hospital and numerous factories, it attracted a diverse population including large numbers of Germans and a small number of Italians and African Americans. By 1912, Edgemont had grown to cover a large area south of Germantown Street and west of the Great Miami River.

RAILROAD CROSSING AT THIRD NEAR MALLEABLE IRON WORKS

Here, a City Railway car makes its way west on Third Street near the Dayton Malleable Iron Works, located on the north side of West Third between Paul Laurence Dunbar and Dale Streets. City Railway, organized in 1893, was a consolidation of several street railway companies. The building partially visible on the left side of the photograph is the Pennsylvania Line and Dayton and Union Railroad Depot. The single overhead streetcar wire was controversial during this period; many feared the electricity would run into the ground, contaminating the groundwater.

CLOSELY TRIMMED TREES AT BROWN AND GREEN STREETS

Oregon, Dayton's first suburb, began development in the 1830s. Located adjacent to downtown, it was within easy walking distance in an era that offered limited public transportation. Unlike later suburbs with wide yards and generous setbacks from the street, Oregon's houses sat bunched together and close to the sidewalk. Backyards for recreational purposes were almost unknown until the late nineteenth century; until the arrival of indoor plumbing and city services this space was largely reserved to meet the sanitary necessities of life, including privies and garbage disposal.

HOUSE AT 664 KEOWEE STREET

The great flood that occurred in the spring of 1913 left in its wake a city that, in the words of one citizen, was "just a great waste of muddy slime, ruins and wreckage." Daytonians returned to a vastly altered streetscape, filled with houses smashed or torn from their foundations. Here, a man peers into the window of a flood-ravaged house in North Dayton, which is being held at an angle by adjacent buildings.

SIDE YARD, 279 ALASKA STREET, SEPTEMBER 25, 1912

     This photograph illustrates the ideal yard, meticulously landscaped following Patterson's three cardinal principles of planting, which he referred to as the ABCs of outdoor art: (a) Keep center of lawn open, (b) Plant in masses, and (c) Avoid straight lines. Patterson, determined to teach others proper landscaping methods, developed lectures delivered upon request in cities across the United States. His efforts proved effective, and he eventually became recognized as the "father of the Beautiful Homes movement," which by 1900 was spreading to cities and towns throughout the nation. This home on Alaska Street in Old North Dayton was the home of carpenter Martin Seil and his wife, Theresa.

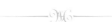

C. D. STEVEN'S BAR, WILLIAMS AND WASHINGTON

The neighborhood saloon was the most important social center for working men until the beginning of prohibition in 1919 robbed them of the pleasure of drinking with their buddies (at least in public). Each bar had its own personality and particular clientele, and this one seemed to be one where a fellow did not have to be much concerned with formality. The state of the floor, indicating only casual use of spittoons, and the dog snoozing at the end of the bar, suggests sanitary conditions that would be unacceptable to today's health inspectors.

MISS PARROTT PUTTING UP FLAG AT FOWLER'S RESIDENCE, JUNE 1913

Flag Day was first celebrated in 1877 in honor of the flag's centennial, and while it did not become an official day of national observance until 1949, it was observed in cities and towns across the nation. The day not only honored the birth of the flag, but was seen as an opportunity to teach children respect for their country. Here, Miss Parrott watches as two children hang the Stars and Stripes in preparation for the celebration.

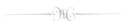

BELLMONTE AVENUE, SEPTEMBER 12, 1912

In 1875, prominent Daytonian John Stoddard submitted a plat for the exclusive Bellmonte Park subdivision, adding extensions in 1890 and 1906. The suburb's idyllic setting, composed of winding streets and wooded lots, quickly filled with the elegant homes of some of the city's wealthiest citizens, including such notables as Thomas Elder, Edwin Reynolds, and Richard Burkhardt. This photo shows Bellmonte Avenue (today spelled "Belmonte") still in the early stages of development. The area (the location of the Dayton Art Institute) is now known as Grafton Hill.

JEFFERSON STREET CANAL BRIDGE, MARCH 22, 1911

The Miami-Erie Canal formed the western boundary of Oregon, the city's earliest suburb. In the distance are the smokestacks of the eastern industrial district and the Armory, still one of downtown's most architecturally distinctive buildings. At right is Trinity Reformed Church, established in 1886. The massive brick building was completed at the corner of Green and Jefferson Streets in 1894.

BILLBOARDS BETWEEN THIRD AND DALE, CIRCA 1916

Billboards proliferated in the twentieth century as businesses vied for the growing consumer dollar. Here, the Ringling Brothers advertise the "World's Greatest Shows," Prince Albert promises pipe smokers "gobs of joy in every puff," and Camel touts the now famous camel design. Already many Daytonians, including John Patterson, were viewing the latest trend in advertising as yet another blight on the urban landscape. This photo was undoubtedly taken by an NCR photographer to show the deleterious effect of these billboards on the appearance of the Gem City.

MRS. JOHN KISSLING'S CIGAR WAGONS

This photograph showcases the three neatly painted wagons of Mrs. John Kissling, each equipped with a shiny, new and completely glass-encased National cash register. In the background is her confectionery and cigar store, established at the southwest corner of Brown and K Streets in 1911. The clever advertising in the window reading "Get a Permit to Smoke" is a word play on the "Permit" brand of cigar. The building to the right of the store is NCR Building 2.

BROWN STREET LOOKING NORTH FROM WYOMING

This street scene, showing the rough and broken surface of Brown Street, was used in a 1919 publication urging voters to pass a three million dollar city bond issue for Community Betterment. One of the primary issues was the poor condition of many city streets, which suffered from the increased weight of the heavy auto trucks that had replaced the lighter hauling vehicles of the nineteenth century. At left is the Old Glory Theater, which advertised itself as the "Home of Screen Supremacy" and "High Class Motion Pictures." At right is Engine Company No. 11.

HAY WAGON ON EAST THIRD STREET, MAY 1913

In May 1913, NCR photographers took a large number of photographs throughout the city to illustrate to Daytonians and the outside world the city's successful recovery from the 1913 flood. Here, a teamster hauls a wagonload of hay through city streets to provide feed for the horse population, still an important part of urban transportation in the early years of the twentieth century.

WASHINGTON STREET AND RAILROAD CROSSING, APRIL 24, 1911

As Dayton's industries grew, so did the amount of rail traffic coming into the city. The hazardous grade crossings became a growing source of controversy; newspapers carried graphic accounts of the many tragic accidents, as well as demands to build elevated tracks. One of the most controversial crossings was on Washington Street in Edgemont, where NCR had petitioned to be allowed to build a feeder line to provide rail access for the company. The argument over grade crossings would continue unabated until track elevation began in the late 1920s; the first train passed over the elevated tracks at Union Station on December 15, 1930.

at

WORK

Dayton has already established an enviable reputation for the

superior quality of all work done here. The great variety of manufacturing done here

will make it comparatively easy to start industries.

Skilled artisans are at hand, and the fact that Dayton is located very near to the center

of population, together with other natural advantages,

makes her material prosperity assured.

JOHN H. PATTERSON, 1896

When men come to realize that we as a people must progress together,

that one set of men can not prosper unless the common run of men prosper,

there is hope that the industrial millennium is not far off.

DAYTON DAILY NEWS, JANUARY 28, 1915

Known as "the city of a thousand factories," Dayton was an urban center with a diverse industrial base, offering skilled jobs to its rapidly expanding work force. The National Cash Register Company, the Davis Sewing Machine Company and Dayton Malleable Iron Works were only a few of the large employers competing for the services of the city's work force. The new century brought even more opportunities with the establishment of new corporations such as Delco and the Dayton Motor Car Company. Because of the unusually high number of skilled jobs available, Dayton was also known as a "city of home owners," with a high percentage of workers able to buy their own homes. The good life was not open to all; this was a period of narrowing economic opportunities for blacks. Employment for African Americans was for the most part limited to more dangerous industrial tasks, such as unskilled foundry jobs, or to janitorial or domestic work.

Of course, not all Daytonians were employed in industry. They followed many other pursuits, building roads, clerking in stores, delivering groceries, tending to the sick and the poor, teaching children, and doing every other job that was necessary to keep the modern city running smoothly. It was also a period when more professional opportunities were becoming available to women, as teaching and nursing became socially acceptable careers for those of the fairer sex.

To promote the adoption of his worker welfare programs, Patterson instructed NCR photographers to capture both good and bad conditions in the city's factories, contrasting the unsightly conditions at the Dayton Malleable Iron Company, for example, with the neatly kept grounds of the more progressive Davis Sewing Machine Company. Patterson was involved in many aspects of civic reform; therefore, images of street paving, a long fought for accomplishment, appear frequently, as well as demonstrations of new state-of-the-art fire equipment, a must for minimizing fire losses in the modern city. Lastly, Patterson's visual record of those forward-looking businesses which had recently purchased new National cash registers show us Dayton at work in a wide variety of jobs across the community.

CENTRAL UNION SWITCHBOARD

The Central Union Telephone Company was established in Dayton in 1879, and began operation with ten subscribers in August of that year. It was known as the Bell Company and was the city's first telephone company. By 1909, the company was serving 10,350 customers from its location on Ludlow Street between Second and Third. According to local chronicler Charlotte Reeve Conover, Daytonians, especially those approached to become stockholders, initially viewed the telephone as a questionable investment, stating that "it was only an experiment after all, their money was safer in the bank, and that Dayton would never be large enough to make it a really paying investment."

PAVING STEWART STREET, WORKMEN HEATING SMOOTHING IRONS,
MAY 27, 1902

Although many have credited the coming of the automobile with the paving of city streets, the push for good pavement was actually led by bicycling enthusiasts imperiled by slick surfaces and large chuck holes, and by citizens who simply tired of being ankle-deep in sticky mud. Dayton was slow to pave streets; indeed, Daytonians grew so exasperated with the inaction of city government that they formed the Committee of One Hundred, a group of citizens who brought about paving and other improvements. Interestingly, the first paving was done toward the outskirts of town, where property owners did not have enough wealth and influence to effectively protest the heavy street assessments. Paving began in 1889; by 1909 Dayton had fifty-eight miles of paved streets.

NCR TYPEWRITING DEPARTMENT

Not until the 1870s did women begin to invade the all-male domain of the business office. It was the typewriter that provided this entry, as many men felt that women's nimble fingers were better able to operate this new office machine. The women thus occupied were called "typewriters," and they learned their skills in business schools, at the YWCA, or in the new courses offered by up-to-date high schools. By 1900, women filled more than one-third of the clerical jobs, and by 1920 the number increased to one-half. While women at NCR worked in what we would call "typing pool" positions, they were rarely used as personal secretaries or stenographers. Those positions, which offered employees the opportunity for advancement to executive ranks, were not considered suitable for females.

Here, young women "typewriters" work in the pleasant environment provided by the company. Patterson never missed an opportunity to spread his ideas on worker welfare; the large "It Pays" signs hanging from the ceiling reminded factory visitors that healthy working conditions made good, sound economic sense.

PORTER AT TRAIN AT UNION STATION

Porters, especially those that worked for the Pullman Company, included some of the most respected members of the black community. The steady work allowed these men to buy homes and secure good educations for their children, but it also subjected them to long hours, low wages, and unfair employment practices. Although many had college degrees, they still had to adopt a subservient demeanor in order to retain their jobs and to attract the tips needed to subsidize inadequate salaries. Eventually, they turned to union organization to improve their working conditions; in 1925 Asa Philip Randolph founded the Brotherhood of Sleeping Car Porters. After years of struggle, the Pullman Company recognized the union in 1937, making the BSCP the first African American labor union to win a collective bargaining agreement with an American corporation. The Brotherhood would spawn a core of black leaders who would play significant roles in the later Civil Rights movement.

NCR INVENTIONS DEPARTMENT

Charles F. Kettering began his career in Inventions Department No. 3 of The National Cash Register Company in July 1904. One of his accomplishments was the development of the O.K. Charge Phone, which combined the telephone with the cash register and a magnetic stamping device activated from a department store's credit office to authorize a charge. This invention made the cash register effective in department stores, thereby opening a large and lucrative market to the company. Charles Kettering stands at center beside an O.K. Charge Phone and a department store register, which did not at all resemble what we think of as the typical cash register of the period.

DELCO

The Dayton Engineering Laboratories Company, known as Delco, was organized by Charles F. Kettering and Edward A. Deeds in 1910 to produce an electric starter and ignition system for automobiles. The starter first appeared on the 1912 Cadillac, and was immediately successful. Delco was purchased by United Motors in 1916. In 1918, the United Motors Corporation was sold to General Motors.

LAUNDRY GIRL SPRINKLING, OTHERS IRONING, JUNE 27, 1904

By 1900, NCR operated the largest industrial laundry in the world, washing and pressing the thousands of aprons, sleevelets, tablecloths, napkins and other items needed each month for the clean and efficient operation of the company. This photo shows some women working at mangles (ironing machines often used for sheets and tablecloths), while others wield heavy hand irons warmed by a heat source installed at the end of the ironing board. The department is overseen by a forewoman, seated at a desk at the front of the room where she can easily keep her eyes on the young women under her supervision.

DAYTON SAVINGS AND TRUST COMPANY, CIRCA 1922

The Dayton Savings and Trust Company at 25 North Main Street was formed in 1903 and opened in 1904. It was one of the first savings and trust companies in Dayton, and offered services not available in the national banks dominating the city's banking scene during this period. This photograph was taken to document the installation of an NCR Class 2000 accounting machine, a new product that would continue to be very profitable for NCR until the 1970s.

SHOE REPAIR SHOP, LUDLOW STREET, OCTOBER 9, 1913

This photograph shows a shoe repair shop typical of the early twentieth century. There is no cash register in evidence, which was the usual reason for NCR to photograph a shop interior. Perhaps the photo was taken to illustrate that business continued as usual despite the flood that damaged or destroyed most of downtown just seven months earlier.

INTERIOR DURST MILLING COMPANY, 1904

The company began as Ludlow Mills in 1868, becoming Banner Mills in 1879, and Durst Milling Company in 1887. This interior view shows employees busy with the many tasks involved in the operation of the business. A large, newly installed National cash register occupies center stage in the photograph, taken to show the use of a cash register in a milling operation. The Durst Milling Company was located at 303–315 East Fifth Street.

THE DAYTON MOTOR CAR COMPANY SHOP, EAST THIRD STREET

The company began as a farm implement manufacturer in 1869, and was reorganized as The Stoddard Manufacturing Company in 1884. Sensing the future profitability of the new auto industry, the Company began to produce automobiles in 1903. The automobile quickly displaced the manufacture of farm implements, and The Dayton Motor Car Company was organized in 1904. The Stoddard-Dayton quickly became known throughout the United States, Canada and South America; one Daytonian told a story of an acquaintance who had the startling experience of coming face-to-face with a Stoddard automobile in a remote village in the Andes Mountains in 1909. The Dayton Motor Car Company became part of the United States Motor Company in 1910. Production of the Stoddard stopped in 1913, but the plant was retained for assembly of the Maxwell 35. A part of this manufacturing complex still stands at East Third and Bainbridge Streets.

NCR ART DEPARTMENT, AUGUST 3, 1900

When John and Frank Patterson purchased the cash register business in 1884, they bought the machine that nobody wanted. John Patterson, the more imaginative of the two brothers, immediately launched an aggressive direct mail advertising campaign so intense that one merchant wrote back and pleaded with him to let up, as he had never done anything to Patterson to merit the unsolicited barrage of materials. The use of "educational advertising" (creating a market for a product by teaching the potential customer why he needed it) was unheard of except in the patent medicine business. John Patterson—ever the imaginative adapter of others' ideas—adapted their methods to selling the cash register. At first everybody thought he was crazy (people frequently thought John was crazy), but as his success turned from modest to phenomenal his detractors quit laughing and started copying his methods. Here, NCR ad men are hard at work, designing the colorful and verbally commanding advertising pieces that helped make the company a world-wide success.

DAVIS SEWING MACHINE COMPANY

The Davis Sewing Machine Company was organized at Watertown, New York in 1868 and relocated to Dayton's east side off Linden Avenue in 1888. By 1909, the factory had grown to occupy over fourteen acres of floor space and produced over 250,000 sewing machines annually. In 1895, the company began to manufacture bicycles. Known as the "Dayton bicycle," the new product was an immediate success, and the company eventually became Huffy Corporation, the world's largest bicycle producer. The airy and well-lit factory located on tastefully landscaped grounds was probably photographed by an NCR photographer as an example of one of the city's model manufacturing establishments.

DAYTON MALLEABLE IRON WORKS, DECEMBER 4, 1912

The Dayton Malleable Iron Works was established in 1866 on Dayton's east side by Charles Newbold and Peter Loeb. In 1872, the company relocated to Third Street on the city's west side; by 1909 the work force had grown to 1,500 laborers. Dirty and unattractive, bordered by streets lined with piles of debris, the factory was likely photographed as one of Dayton's "unsightly places." Many of the factories of the period shared this unpleasant aesthetic, and Patterson campaigned zealously to prove to manufacturers that it paid in dollars and cents to provide clean and pleasant surroundings to factory employees.

GEBHART-WUICHET COMPANY, PLANER IN SHOP, NOVEMBER 28, 1913

  The Gebhart-Wuichet planing mills were located at Fourth and Wyandot Streets in Dayton's busy eastern industrial district, which extended eastward from the Miami-Erie Canal (now Patterson Boulevard). Business was probably booming for this lumber company as workers raced to fill the heavy demand for building materials created by the 1913 flood just seven months earlier.

MAN POURING OFF, NCR FOUNDRY, NOVEMBER 14, 1919

In the early twentieth century, African Americans migrated to northern industrial cities in ever increasing numbers seeking better lives for themselves and their families. Foundry work, one of the "3H" jobs (hot, heavy and hard), was one of the few occupations open to African American males, who faced narrowing economic opportunities in the first decades of the 1900s.

ZINK'S BUTCHER SHOP IN ARCADE, CIRCA 1913

John I. Zink operated this butcher shop in the Third Street Arcade from 1911 to 1914. He also operated a restaurant at 42 South Ludlow. The uncovered trays of meat on the counter and the scrap bucket beneath the wooden butcher block are a reminder of how much public health standards have changed. The large scale at center was made by the Computing Scale Company, the first computing scale company in the world. The photo was taken to show the use of a National cash register in a butcher shop.

ROBERT MALLORY'S HOTEL AND BAR, LUDLOW AND THE RAILROAD

Robert A. Mallory, one of Dayton's leading citizens, owned the Mallory Hotel at 314 South Ludlow Street. He and his wife, Flora, made their home in the spacious two-story brick house at 803 West Fifth Street. Their son was Captain Robert H. Mallory, who, as director of Linden Center, would be instrumental in attaining the funding needed to build the well-equipped modern community center that still stands on Norwood Avenue on the West Side. Here, Mr. Mallory and friends pose for an NCR photographer.

UNLOADING MOVING VAN, LOWES STREET, FEBRUARY 1915

      Then, as now, Americans were a mobile people, moving from home to home to accommodate changes in family size, jobs and economic circumstances. In this photograph, a mover carries a heavy settee into this modest Victorian home on Lowes Street. Jacob Young's Sons moving company was located on Hickory Street in the South Park neighborhood, and advertised themselves as the owners of "the largest auto truck in Dayton."

WOMAN PICKING UP COAL, RAILROAD NEAR TAYLOR

Coal was the primary fuel used for cooking and heating in turn of the century America. This photograph captures a rare image of a woman scavenging coal in the city's rail yard on a cold winter's day. It was likely taken to illustrate the continuing hardships faced by many Daytonians, who had yet to share in the growing prosperity of the period.

MOVING A HOUSE OFF MAIN STREET TO MAKE ROOM
FOR NEW NCR FACTORY BUILDINGS, MAY 23, 1900

NCR hired Peter P. Muth & Sons to remove buildings standing in the way of factory expansion. Here, several men work without the benefit of motorized equipment to maneuver a house to its new location. Muth & Sons specialized in moving houses and heavy machinery and began operation in 1890.

G. W. SHROYER AND COMPANY, OCTOBER 5, 1910

The wholesale and retail business of G. W. Shroyer at the northeast corner of Main and Second offered an amazing variety of merchandise, including bicycles, automobiles, sporting goods, cameras and phonographs. Today, it would be unthinkable for automobiles to be marketed in a sporting goods store, but in that period the lack of a well-established system of car dealerships meant that autos were sometimes sold in what to us would be the most unlikely places.

U. S. MAIL WAGON, SOUTH SIDE BUILDING 10, MARCH 16, 1908

In 1908, NCR was still receiving its large mail deliveries by horse-drawn wagon, despite the fact that the Post Office had begun to make the transition to motorized vehicles in 1901. The first twenty years of the new century would bring radical changes in postal delivery; the first government-owned motor vehicle service was established in 1914 and airmail was begun in 1918. The rate of change is particularly amazing when one realizes that when this photo was made in 1908, the United States still owned only one airplane. Here, a postal worker poses with his horse and wagon outside of NCR's Building 10.

NCR FINAL INSPECTION, OCTOBER 13, 1905

NCR took great pride in turning out high-quality cash registers, carefully inspecting machines for possible flaws before shipping them to purchasers. The company produced an endless variety of registers, and was willing to custom-equip them according to the wants and whims of individual customers. In this photo, factory workers (neatly dressed in white shirts and ties) give cash registers a thorough inspection under the watchful eye of the department foreman.

at
PLAY

We should make it assured that the growth of Dayton will never shut off

the children of future generations from access to the grass and trees and open-air sports.

All vacant lots which now disfigure the city will be used for

children's playgrounds or flower gardens.

JOHN H. PATTERSON, 1896

It is now an established fact that no municipality can afford to neglect opportunity to

provide for the boys and girls every possible chance to enjoy

out-of-door life under supervised and systematic efforts. The old corner lot, the alley

and the public thoroughfares which in their time served in a way to provide children with

a place to play, are thoroughly discredited now for this purpose.

The city needs to keep its program for public playgrounds in mind at all times.

There must be no recession from our plans for development.

DAYTON DAILY NEWS, MARCH 14, 1923

Life could be challenging in the busy industrial city, and hardworking Daytonians turned to recreation to escape the pressures of everyday life. Horse races continued to be well-attended, but citizens also adopted a myriad of new activities. Baseball, played in army camps during the Civil War, grew in popularity. Boys transformed vacant lots into makeshift ball diamonds, while men organized into workplace teams, competing in citywide leagues with friends and family providing exuberant support from the sidelines.

Daytonians took to the roads via the bicycle, which became a favored leisure activity after the invention of the safety wheel in the 1880s. In good weather, Sunday crowds of cyclists braved the mud and dust of city and county roads to picnic at sylvan retreats on the city's edge. The coming of the automobile in the early twentieth century gave birth to the automobile club, which sponsored special events for auto enthusiasts in the nascent days of America's love affair with the automobile. New sports such as tennis and golf quickly found favor, while canoeing and camping offered further opportunities for exercise and fresh air. Swimming became more formalized; while boys continued to sneak a cool dip in the dirty waters of the Miami-Erie Canal, safe and sanitary swimming environments such as the inside pool at the YMCA helped discourage the use of the rivers and canal. Street fairs and circuses drew crowds searching for pleasant diversions from everyday routines, and theaters offering vaudeville acts and the new moving pictures took people out of the front parlor and off the front porch and put them into more formal places of entertainment.

Progressive-minded Daytonians increasingly pushed for supervised play areas for children, establishing parks and playgrounds, while in the schools team sports, gymnasiums and playgrounds became an expected part of the modern, up-to-date school. Recreation, a term unknown to earlier generations of Daytonians, had finally come of age.

BARNUM AND BAILEY ANNEX TENT, FAIRGROUNDS

Few events were anticipated with as much excitement as the day the circus came to town. Barnum & Bailey made numerous visits to Dayton, dazzling audiences with their menagerie of exotic animals and amazing feats of daring presented against a backdrop of music, lights and brilliant color. On circus day, hundreds of Daytonians rose early to watch the circus trains unload, and then followed the procession to the fairgrounds to see the army of workers raise the tent city. Later that day, they gathered under the big top, to enjoy the breathtaking spectacle known as "The Greatest Show on Earth."

TWO WOMEN IN AUTOMOBILE

The coming of the automobile diminished the popularity of the bicycle (at its height in the 1890s) and increased city dwellers' opportunities for leisurely escapes to the countryside. The number of autos nationwide rose from 300 in 1895 to 78,000 in 1905, and to 2,446,000 in 1915. This car has a crank starter which tended to discourage women from getting behind the wheel, but the widespread adoption of the electric starter (invented by Charles F. Kettering) in 1913–1914 quickly put large numbers of women drivers on the road.

BOYS PLAYING BASEBALL, 1898

Baseball, which first appeared in eastern cities in the 1840s, quickly grew in popularity, gradually edging out boxing as the favorite American spectator sport. Cincinnati launched the first professional team in 1869, but amateur municipal and industrial leagues also attracted large crowds, who turned out to cheer for co-workers, friends and family members. Vacant lots across the city were instantly transformed into ball diamonds by neighborhood boys, who were always ready to organize a game with or without the proper equipment or number of players. Participants saw the game as good clean fun, but it was assigned a higher purpose by reformers, who proclaimed it an excellent source of physical conditioning and mental discipline, and who saw in the practice of good sportsmanship the ideal way of imbuing city youth with principles of justice.

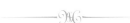

STEWART STREET BICYCLE SHEDS, SEPTEMBER 21, 1910

NCR provided bicycle sheds to encourage their employees to utilize this healthful mode of transportation to get to and from work. Bicycling demanded a change in women's fashions, giving birth to the divided skirt, which, according to historian Charlotte Reeve Conover, "was the first intimation that women were entitled to the use of their legs." Ministers and newspaper editors railed against this lowering of the standard of decency and predicted the decline of the home and the collapse of the universe. But women ignored these dire predictions and continued to enjoy their new freedom of dress, which would only increase as time moved on.

GRAND AMERICAN HANDICAP, GENERAL VIEW SHOWING TRAPS

The first NCR Gun Club was established around 1895 by a group of company employees, and in 1905 the NCR Men's Welfare Work League Gun Club was organized. The men successfully lobbied the company to build a clubhouse and began accepting members outside of the work force. In 1913 and 1914, the Grand American Handicap was held at the NCR Gun Club. John Patterson provided elaborate accommodations for the shooters, including bleachers, dining facilities, a first aid tent, and a barbershop. Many have said that Patterson's overwhelming hospitality was a primary factor in the decision to permanently locate the Amateur Trapshooting Association in nearby Vandalia in 1924.

GROUP OF HORSES IN FAIRGROUNDS, APRIL 29, 1917

The distinctive board-and-batten-sided octagonal building was erected in 1874 by the Southern Fair Association, and today remains the most unique feature of the Montgomery County fairgrounds. Patterson took a great interest in the fairgrounds, located just a stone's throw away from the NCR factory, but saw them as a poorly maintained and under-utilized community asset. He complained that the grounds were not developed for the wider benefit of the people, stating that "horses and mules had for twenty years trampled down the grass and reclined under the shade trees, while the working man had no place where he could take his family and eat his Sunday lunch under a tree without fear of molestation."

WOMEN GOLFERS AT THE DAYTON COUNTRY CLUB

The game of golf was brought to the United States from Scotland in 1888, and led to the establishment of golf courses and country clubs all across the nation. The golf fever quickly spread to Dayton where, according to Charlotte Reeve Conover, "clubs and balls were imported and an occasional cow pasture was made dangerous to its natural inhabitants." In 1898, the Dayton Golf Club was built on a part of the old Patterson Homestead. This image shows the ladies trying their hand at the new sport at the Dayton Country Club, which succeeded the Dayton Golf Club in 1909. The city's women took the sport seriously and were early competitors; in 1920 eight Dayton women competed in the first annual state golf tournament sponsored by the Ohio Women's Golf Association.

ENTRANCE TO AUTO CLUB, 1912

Americans were quick to take advantage of the opportunities the automobile offered for new types of recreation. Auto clubs sprang up everywhere, staging road races and organizing "gymkhanas" at county fairgrounds. The clubs also lobbied for better roads and added their voices to the development of traffic rules and regulations. Patterson established the Dayton Auto Club on the old Coblentz farm south of the city, converting the house and barn to a clubhouse. In this photo, members speed through the club entrance, cheered on by a crowd of excited spectators.

BALL GAME AT McKINLEY PARK, MAY 13, 1916

McKinley Park (located across from the Dayton Art Institute) was one of many recreational green spaces established in Dayton in the early twentieth century. The city's park movement was given a tremendous boost in 1907 when Patterson threatened to move his "model factory of the world" if parks and other civic improvements were not speedily forthcoming. Now, it seemed unthinkable that Patterson would abandon his large and beautiful factory complex, but then you never really knew. Patterson had proved on more than one occasion that he was quite capable of acting quickly, decisively and dramatically when he decided that the situation warranted it. Not wanting to push him too far, city officials agreed to his list of demands for progress.

McKinley Park was devastated by the 1913 flood and was further blighted by its use as an official dumping ground for flood debris. Its fall from beauty was temporary; by 1916 the park had regained much of its former charm and was again the site of baseball games and other community activities.

NCR MEN'S WELFARE WORK LEAGUE MAKING BURGOO, OCTOBER 1, 1904

A crowd of nine thousand filled the fairgrounds on Saturday, October 1, 1904 to attend the barbecue given by the Men's Welfare Work League. Men, women and children enjoyed roast beef and burgoo, a stew of meat and vegetables, and watched a series of athletic events, including a football game between the NCR team and the Jacobs Business College Eleven. This photo shows League members hard at work stirring the heavy iron kettles.

YOUNG LADIES PLAYING TENNIS, JULY 1904

The game of tennis was adopted from the British in the mid-1870s, and became a favored lawn sport in America by the mid-1880s. Popular among the young fashionable set who could afford to pay for membership in private clubs, the game assumed a more public dimension when some cities made courts a feature of public parks about 1900. NCR provided courts to employees and most likely made them available to those who lived in the neighborhood. The women here seem unhampered by their long dresses, which must have been hot and awkward in the heavy summer heat.

NCR DANCING CLASS

NCR offered a wide variety of classes to its employees, but none were as well-attended as the company's dancing classes. Dancing was a favorite leisure-time pursuit in this period, and dances were held at private clubs and public places across the city. City officials had so many problems maintaining public decorum in local dance halls that they finally published photographs in the Dayton Daily News, illustrating proper and improper dance postures and warning that: "Putting your cheek up against your partner's, shimmying, head-to-head, pivoting and all the other holds of the modern terpsichorean wrestlers are tabooed under a recent ruling of [City] Safety Director Myers."

HORSE RACE, MONTGOMERY COUNTY FAIRGROUNDS, SEPTEMBER 8, 1904

Horse racing, always popular with Daytonians (even on city streets), began to be an important attraction at the county fair after the Southern Fair Association enlarged the race track at the Montgomery County fairgrounds in the 1870s. Here, spectators fill the grandstand and line the fence to observe a harness racing event. The NCR factory is in the background.

DAYTON STREET FAIR, McKINLEY CLUB SIDE SHOW, SEPTEMBER 9, 1901

Street fairs promised viewers a wide range of attractions from fascinating oddities to lurid monstrosities. Although some social reformers considered them a cultural (although temporary) blight on the urban landscape, they continued to attract crowds of curious urbanites and country dwellers eager for a brief respite from the challenges of every day life.

C. P. RODGERS IN HIS BIPLANE AT THE NCR COUNTRY CLUB, 1911

Calbraith Perry Rodgers was the first aviator to fly a plane across the width of the United States. It was not without incident; out of the forty-nine days it took him to complete the flight only three days, ten hours and four minutes were actually spent in the air. The remainder of the time was spent recovering from the sixteen crashes which interrupted his original flight plan. John Patterson early on grasped the possibilities of flight, supporting the efforts of the Wright brothers and other early aviators and working diligently to make Dayton the center of aeronautical research and development.

THE COLUMBIA THEATER

The Columbia, located on South Jefferson between Third and Fourth Streets, was the city's most elegant theater when it opened in 1914. Its somewhat exotic exterior was enticing to passersby, who crowded into the 500-seat theater. Here, colorful broadsides advertise the current feature films, while a sign on the adjacent building touts Monday showings of "Pathé's Weekly," one of the country's earliest sources of news film.

BASEBALL FIELD SOUTH OF FACTORY, SEPTEMBER 14, 1907

Large industrial plants, such as NCR, established dozens of baseball teams during the period to encourage teamwork and to lessen labor tensions. These industrial leagues were very competitive; some companies actually went so far as to raid the minor leagues, paying players big salaries to work in the factory during the week and to play Saturday and Sunday ball with the company team. So far as is known, however, NCR did not take part in these questionable practices. This photo shows a game at the ball field behind Building 10. The twenty-five foot high "NCR" sign on top of the ten-story office building was erected in the fall of 1906, and was the largest electric sign in the world.

TAYLOR STREET BETWEEN FIRST AND SECOND, MARCH 23, 1912

Among the many new forms of recreation introduced during the last half of the nineteenth century was roller skating. The first roller skates were in-line skates, but the invention of the modern four-wheel roller skate by James Leonard Plimpton in 1863 produced a skate that was easier to control. Skating became the new fad of the mid-1870s, which, in some cities, took place on inside cycling rinks constructed for bicyclists who preferred to avoid the hazardous road conditions of the period. In Dayton, skaters competed for sizeable cash prizes at Lakeside Park Roller Skating Rink in front of large crowds of spectators. Here, young skaters stop their sidewalk cruise to pose for an NCR photographer.

HILLS AND DALES PLAYGROUND, CIRCA 1915

Sandboxes originated in Germany, where sand heaps were first placed in Berlin to provide recreation for children. The first sandbox in America was built in Boston in 1886. They caught on rapidly; soon sandboxes appeared in parks and playgrounds in cities and towns across the nation. The earliest sandboxes, like the one in the photo, had wooden frames with no fixed bottoms. Social reformers considered that sandboxes transferred children's play from the gravel and gutters of the street to a sanitary, educational setting, and fostered creative play in city children.

PLAYING PUSHBALL AT THE COUNTRY CLUB IN DAYTON, SEPTEMBER 22, 1912

That sports on horseback were much admired by Daytonians was reflected in the words of a contemporary Dayton Daily News writer who declared: "Polo is a man's game. Red-blooded courage, daring hazardousness, expert horsemanship, a steady nerve and a good set of muscles, well-trained, are requisite. It is not brutal; it is manly. It is not cruel; it is entrancing." That being said, this photograph is not about polo; it's about pushball on which information was elusive. It may have been a version of a game called "pushball" which appeared in the early twentieth century and was played on foot between two opposing teams. Perhaps these Dayton horsemen simply conducted their pushball game on horseback.

MR. DEEDS' CAR LOADED WITH PONY GOING TO SPRINGFIELD HORSE SHOW

Edward Deeds (not pictured) came to NCR in 1899 as a young electrical engineer. He left the company in 1909 to co-found Delco with Charles F. Kettering, returning to NCR in 1931 as chairman of the board. Deeds took a leading role in flood prevention, serving from 1915 to 1954 as president of the Miami Conservancy District. He was instrumental in Dayton's development as a center of aviation. It is certainly hard to imagine putting a pony in this elegant Packard automobile, but the photograph shows the pony loaded up and ready for transport.

NEIGHBORHOOD WADING POOL, AUGUST 1915

The wading pool, located on L Street, was built by The National Cash Register Company in 1915 to offer a safe and fun way for children to escape the intense heat of Dayton summers. Later, the company would again expand its recreational facilities when, under the direction of Edward Deeds, NCR built Old River Park during the Great Depression of the 1930s.

THE ROUND CAMP, HILLS AND DALES

Patterson began buying land for the creation of Hills & Dales Park in 1905 as a rustic retreat for employees and their families. He quickly added bridle paths and roads as well as a clubhouse, camp sites, tennis courts, a golf course and baseball diamonds. The camps were modeled after his summer camp in the Adirondacks. In 1918, he donated the park to the city for the enjoyment of all Daytonians, contributing $10,000 a year for the next three years for upkeep. Here, campers enjoy an outing at the Round Camp.

DAY NURSERY PICNIC, UNLOADING CHILDREN FROM AUTO, JUNE 9, 1913

As the number of women working outside the home increased, so did the need for childcare. Patterson, who believed in the importance of early childhood education and supervised recreation, provided a company day nursery, hiring teachers trained in the most up-to-date instructional methods. In this photo, children are helped down from this open-air vehicle under the watchful eye of their teacher, who is waving a cautioning finger at her young charges.

EDUCATION

Men are happiest where there is the most widespread education.

JOHN H. PATTERSON, 1896

Teachers and students are realizing the advantage of proper exercise and of the discipline
which follows the training in athletics. It is to be hoped that the
tendency will be followed until every child in every public school is given a regular course
in athletic training, along with the mental exercises which are furnished.

DAYTON DAILY NEWS, JUNE 2, 1915

The turn of the century brought a cultural flowering to Dayton. The "club movement," which began in the late 1880s, gave birth to countless self-improvement and discussion clubs for men and women. In particular, clubs offered women the first-time opportunity to admit interest in something other than the home and church and to meet for mutual self-improvement. Initially literary in character, the women's clubs quickly expanded their purpose, lobbying for such civic and social improvements as juvenile courts and public playgrounds, and even reaching out to provide a wide range of philanthropic services such as the preparation of hot lunches for factory girls.

It was in these years that the city's educational system assumed much of the form it has today. Concerns over child labor and the desire to remove mischievous young boys from city streets and vacant lots encouraged the passage of compulsory attendance laws and the extension of the school year. Graded classes and professionally trained teachers gave more structure to the schools, while the changing needs of the growing city with its expanding industrial base caused a radical transformation in curricula. Science classes, accounting, home economics and manual training were added to prepare young minds for work in Dayton's businesses and industries. Kindergarten was introduced, its concept of directed play used to enliven the teaching process throughout the primary grades. Modern school buildings were built, equipped with the latest in sanitary facilities, heat and lighting, libraries, laboratories, assembly rooms and gymnasiums. Throughout the period, the schools assumed more responsibility for the formation of good character, and extracurricular activities and sports were added to teach the value of cooperative action and team play.

As the public demanded more and more services, school buildings frequently acted as community social centers, furnishing much needed space for adult education, vacation schools and other activities. A wide range of night classes held in locations across the city offered adults the chance to make up for their previous lack of educational opportunities and to increase their ability to make a living. Expanded library services, including branch libraries, provided additional educational resources for children and adults. By the end of the period, the modern educational system had emerged, leaving a progressive city at its zenith ready to take on the challenges of the new century.

WARD RATIONAL READING, SCHILLER SCHOOL, FIRST GRADE

School reforms, begun in the years following the Civil War, accelerated in the 1890s, with the introduction of many new teaching methods. In this photograph, students learn to read using Ward Rational Reading, a phonics method introduced in 1896 by educator Edward G. Ward, Superintendent of Public Instruction in Brooklyn, New York. Schiller School, originally known as the Nineteenth District School, was erected in 1895 at the corner of Dover and Bidleman Streets.

STEELE HIGH SCHOOL, INCORRIGIBLE CLASS, JUNE 10, 1912

This photograph shows that the presence of overly exuberant boys in the classroom is not a new problem. In this period, Dayton educators dealt with the problem by labeling them "incorrigible" and keeping them busy, in this instance by making rugs. Two boys by the wall prepare materials for the loom, while two others are occupied weaving. The boys seem undaunted by their unflattering label—the smiles on their faces suggest they may have even prided themselves on it.

STIVERS HIGH SCHOOL, MANUAL TRAINING CLASS IN HOUSE FRAMING, 1914

The first American manual training school, modeled after the Russian Imperial Technical School, opened in St. Louis in 1880. It recognized the urgent need for a new kind of education that would provide the large numbers of highly skilled laborers essential to a rapidly industrializing society. Although initially viewed with suspicion by labor leaders, who feared that the school would breed a generation of strikebreakers, the concept was warmly embraced by business leaders. Dayton's first manual training school opened in January 1896. At first, the number of students was small and the facilities were inadequate. Finally, Stivers Manual Training High School, fitted out with the finest up-to-date equipment, was erected in 1908. Here, students demonstrate their newly acquired skills in house framing.

MILLINERY CLASS IN NCR HOUSE, OCTOBER 1899

This photo shows a group of South Park women hard at work creating artistic hats in a class conducted at the NCR House of Usefulness, a neighborhood center owned and operated by the company. The women are decorating their hats with artificial flowers, a popular trimming of the period. As the new century dawned, millinery would become more and more outlandish, culminating in the Merry Widow, a large brimmed hat trimmed with plumes that came in style in 1907. Church and theater goers bemoaned the arrival of this outrageous fashion; some, in fact, required that the ladies remove their view-blocking headgear. One building owner, offended by the amount of space required, posted a sign reading "Ladies with Merry Widow Hats Take Freight Elevator."

KINDERGARTEN EATING LUNCH ON BACK PORCH

In 1896, Patterson established Dayton's first kindergarten to provide a model for progressive education to the public schools. He believed that the kindergarten principle was a basic one which should be applied everywhere—even in his own factory. The concept was that if you let employees know the expected outcome of their labors and provided the right working environment, they would grow to meet or exceed their employers' expectations. In March of 1899, several hundred delegates of the International Kindergarten Union visited the factory to study the practical application of the kindergarten principle to business. Impressed with what they saw, they declared the NCR factory to be "the most perfect example of a great big business kindergarten." This photo shows the kindergarten children having lunch on the back porch of the NCR House of Usefulness on Stewart Street.

NCR BOYS' GARDENS, SEPTEMBER 1904

Patterson firmly believed that farming instilled a strong work ethic and taught young people how to overcome obstacles. So after he built his sunlight factory buildings with their eighty per cent glass walls, he turned to agriculture to get the neighborhood boys to quit hurling rocks through his gleaming glass windows. In 1897, he began his program of Boys' Gardens; boys were assigned large lots, supplied with seeds and tools, and given guidance and instruction. The youths could take the resulting harvest home to their family or could sell it to earn much-needed cash. Those who successfully completed the multi-year program were awarded certificates and gained entrée into the NCR work force. Later, gardening opportunities were extended to the girls. The program became the most famous of all NCR's worker welfare programs, and was adopted by factories, schools and other organizations across the nation. Here, boy gardeners pose with wagons and baskets filled with produce beside the tool house on Rubicon Street.

STEELE HIGH SCHOOL, EXTERIOR WEST AND NORTH SIDE VIEW, APRIL 25, 1907

Steele High School, located on the southeast corner of Main and Monument, was completed in 1894 and was lauded as the second-best high school building in the United States. Here, NCR shoots motion picture film of an unspecified event from the bed of one of the company's electric trucks. In the spring of 1907, the great Steele lion was not yet standing guard, but it would soon appear, quickly garnering international fame. In a 1909 Paris journal, the bronze lion would be declared to be the finest representation of the American movement to place art in the schools in order to elevate public taste. Paid for through the energetic fundraising efforts of Steele High School students, the lion was sculpted by artist Anna Hyatt.

MEETING OF THE LITERARY SOCIETY AT STEELE HIGH SCHOOL, DECEMBER 10, 1914

The "club movement," which began in the latter years of the nineteenth century, gave women opportunities to meet and discuss the issues of the day. As late as 1890, however, some husbands were still questioning whether a woman's club could be considered respectable. After all, everyone knew that women had nothing really meaningful to discuss or contribute, and they were not real citizens, lacking the power to effect change through action at the polls. Women, as usual, ignored the negative opinions of the opposite sex, testing their wings through the formation of a wide variety of literary and social welfare organizations. African American women joined in the movement, forming numerous clubs that expanded the intellectual horizons of black women. Here, the Society president, gavel in hand, leads the transaction of business of the Literary Society, while the club secretary transcribes the meeting's events.

---※---

PILLARS ARE ADDED TO THE NCR SCHOOLHOUSE, CIRCA 1913

     The NCR Hall of Industrial Education (the Schoolhouse) was completed in the spring of 1912, and immediately became an important center for company and community affairs. Steele High School began the custom of using the facility for graduations when they first held their exercises there in 1924. For years, employees filled the hall for noontime entertainments, and children arrived en masse on Saturday mornings to enjoy the company's special youth programs. The building was expanded in 1913–1914 and again in 1922. In 1938, Colonel Edward Deeds, chairman of the board, renamed it the "NCR Auditorium," in order to avoid confusion with newly completed Building 26, constructed to accommodate night school classes.

WOMEN LEARNING TO VOTE, 1920

After women won the vote, numerous Dayton civic groups organized classes to equip women to exercise their newly acquired right. This photograph, taken October 27, 1920, shows women attending a voting class in the NCR Auditorium. Interestingly, not all women were eager to exercise their voting privilege. In a poll conducted by the Dayton Daily News, only two of thirty women said that they would definitely vote in the upcoming election. According to the reporter, "Ten asserted they don't give a rap about the ballot [and five] said they are too busy attending to household duties to think about voting." An East Third Street woman gave a particularly vehement response stating, "Say, what have I got a husband for? Nothing doing in the voting line—at least yet. I hate to think that the suffragists are forcing an unpleasant duty on me."

PAUL LAURENCE DUNBAR SPEAKING TO NCR EMPLOYEES

This image of Paul Laurence Dunbar is the only known photograph which shows him speaking to an audience. On January 7, 1904 the Dayton Evening News covered Dunbar's visit to The National Cash Register plant, where he gave readings and recitations to hundreds of company employees. His visit was heralded as the "Return of a Hero," the story of a local man who had become an internationally famous literary figure.

DRESS MAKING CLASS, APRIL 24, 1907

NCR offered a wide variety of classes to their women workers to increase their ability to run an efficient, modern household. Here, women are hard at work cutting fabric and assembling dress pieces on the late model sewing machines provided by the company. The white shirtwaists and dark skirts worn by the ladies were the accepted style of dress for working women in turn of the century America. NCR encouraged their female employees to conform to this style, viewing brightly colored or frilly clothing as inappropriate in the workplace.

BOOK WAGON IN NCR FACTORY, 1898

Patterson believed that learning should be a life-long experience, and very early in the company's history established a library stocked with books on an endless number of subjects from health to travel to the mechanical trades. Dissatisfied with the low number of employees taking advantage of the library, he took action to encourage workers to read and expand their range of knowledge. The traveling libraries—books on carts—were wheeled to the entrances of the three main factory buildings so employees no longer had any excuse for not doing some extracurricular reading. Books were loaned for one week for one cent, and could be renewed for an additional week.

WASHINGTON SCHOOL, OPEN AIR PERIOD, DECEMBER 10, 1914

The Twentieth District School, also known as Washington School, was built in 1899 at the corner of Jersey and Sower Streets on Dayton's East Side. A large and elegantly styled school, it was part of a turn of the century program aimed at providing well-equipped modern buildings to meet the educational needs of the growing city. With the new emphasis on child welfare and preventive healthcare, the public schools took on responsibility not only for imparting academic knowledge, but also for safeguarding student health. Despite the chilliness of a December day, the children stand with their hands extended towards the open windows in an effort to rid the classroom of disease-causing germs.

NCR COOKING CLASS AT PATTERSON SCHOOL, APRIL 19, 1906

Patterson believed that workers who were fed healthy, well-prepared meals were more effective both in their work and in their personal life. His efforts to teach others his ideas on nutrition began in 1895 when he treated 200 NCR women employees to a class in cooking and domestic economy at the YWCA as a reward for their improved work performance. From that time onward, the company sponsored cooking classes for both employees and factory neighborhood residents. Here, women learn to prepare a nutritious meal at a cooking class at Patterson School on Wyoming Street near Brown. This school was the scene of many Patterson experiments in progressive education.

ALLEN SCHOOL GARDEN, PLAYGROUND AND GARDEN ASSOCIATION, AUGUST 1913

Dayton's first school garden was established about 1900 when John Patterson convinced Leota Clark, the principal of Patterson School, to busy her students in converting the debris-filled vacant lot adjacent to the school into a garden. Although she and her teachers at first faced "adverse criticism and ridicule," the garden proved to be an immediate success. The Playground and Garden Association later expanded these early efforts, and by 1918 there were eighteen model school gardens. The organization also encouraged adults to become involved in the garden movement; at its peak in 1918 there were 3,600 home gardens and more than 2,000 gardens on vacant lots throughout the city. This photo shows students hard at work in the experimental gardens at Allen School, located in the Old North Dayton neighborhood.

NCR COOKING SCHOOL CLASS, BROOM DRILL IN DINING ROOMS, 1899

Military drill was a popular form of education and recreation in turn of the century American society. It taught order and discipline and was enjoyed by children who participated in large numbers. Here, children of the NCR cooking class practice military drills using brooms instead of weapons. The girls frequently performed at the many NCR sales conventions and other events held by the company.

Educators gradually came to appreciate the value of incorporating the arts into their classroom teaching. Here, a group of cleverly costumed second graders act out "The Piped Piper" in front of an attentive audience of classmates. Irving School, the Thirteenth District School, was located at the corner of Cincinnati and Albany Streets in the Edgemont neighborhood, and was one of four schools erected in Dayton in 1891.

GIRLS IN LIBRARY OF NCR WOMAN'S CENTURY CLUB HOUSE
BROWN AND KIEFABER, APRIL 25, 1904

The Woman's Century Club was organized in April 1896 for the "furtherance of musical, literary, and educational matters," and was composed of all the young women who worked for NCR. Patterson believed that women were the better equipped of the sexes to solve many of the social, moral and educational problems of the day, and used the group to further his agenda. This photograph shows a few members sharing leisure time in the first club house at the corner of Brown and Kiefaber. (In September 1904, the club would relocate to the Patterson Homestead). The gentleman seated at right was probably the Reverend Holmes Whitmore, the pastor of Christ Episcopal Church, who assisted Patterson in carrying out his aggressive program of social reform.

BOYS REPAIRING SHOES, FIRST MUNICIPAL EXHIBIT OF DAYTON, OCTOBER 15, 1915

The First Municipal Exhibit of Dayton was held in October 1915 at Memorial Hall. This ten-day exhibit promoted progressive reform in education and city management, and was a cooperative effort of the Dayton Bureau of Research, the City of Dayton, Montgomery County, and the Dayton Public Schools. Here, two boys demonstrate shoe repair skills learned in Dayton's manual training school.

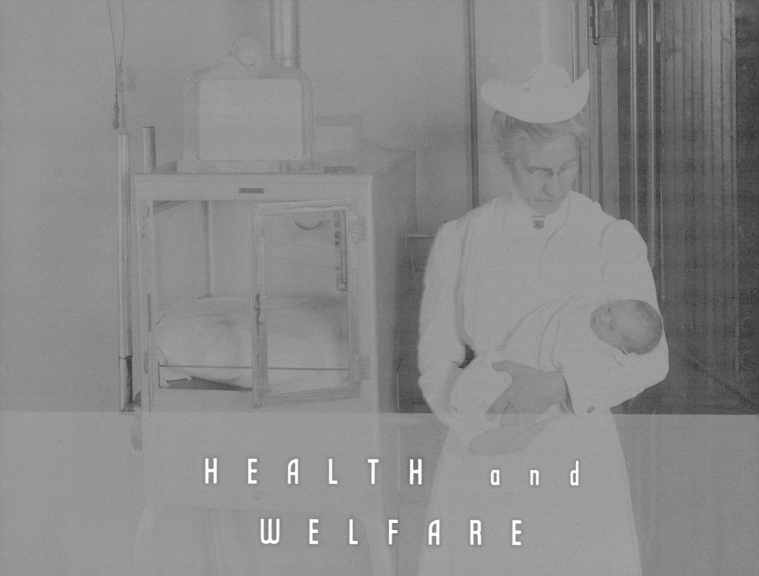

HEALTH and WELFARE

A great many people ask us about our Welfare Work, and why we do it. We do it

because it is right and because it pays. We believe that in doing good for our people we are

raising the standard of workmanship and the standard of morals in

the neighborhood surrounding our plant. Some persons ask 'What is Welfare Work?'

Welfare Work is capital and labor working together for the benefit of

each other, and when capital and labor get behind the wheel of progress, you can bet that

it goes straight ahead, but when they pull opposite to each other, then both are losers.

JOHN H. PATTERSON

Human activities are rapidly being reduced to a science. Living itself is becoming an art.

There is no longer any chance for the individual or for the community that trusts to chance.

Splendid cities have 'sprung up' in the past, without planning. Many men of other days got

along pretty well in a haphazard manner, without applying the laws of science to their affairs.

But that was a thing of the past. The modern city becomes a scientific thing.

DAYTON DAILY NEWS, JUNE 19, 1916

Dayton's rapid growth from a small town of 38,000 to a city of 85,000 in 1900 alarmed citizens, who noted that growth—a source of immense pride to Daytonians—was unfortunately accompanied by an increase in crime, poverty and disease. The city applied its energies and progressive ideals to meeting these challenges. Large private organizations, often with national affiliations, such as the YMCA and YWCA, emerged to become powerful instruments of social change, working alongside countless numbers of small charities to ease the city's growing pains.

Citizens, who were finally beginning to understand the causes of disease, began to realize that "an ounce of prevention is worth a pound of cure," resulting in the formation of the Tuberculosis Commission, the Visiting Nurses Association, the Milk Commission and other organizations. Concern over the welfare of the child brought a system of medical and dental inspections into the schools as well as numerous healthcare programs for children and infants. John Patterson, who was deeply involved in nearly all aspects of social reform, pioneered worker welfare programs at NCR, teaching others that a safe, healthy working environment benefited both employer and employee.

As public problems mounted, citizens demanded that local government expand and exercise its powers for the public good. As a result, city government (especially after the adoption of the city manager form of government in 1914) moved to develop the policies and agencies necessary to safeguard public health and welfare. The modernization of the police and fire departments, construction of streets and sewers, planning and zoning, the operation of public utilities, and the construction of parks and community centers became the responsibility of local government, relieving private agencies from assuming primary responsibility for the community's welfare.

STUART PATTERSON PARK, 1922

Stuart Patterson Park was named in honor of John Patterson's nephew, who was killed in an airplane crash at Wilbur Wright Field on June 19, 1918. Located on Baltimore Street in Old North Dayton, it was one of many city parks established in the early twentieth century to provide safe, supervised recreation areas for urban children.

NCR FIRE DEPARTMENT THROWING WATER BETWEEN BUILDINGS

NCR is said to have been the first American company to have a factory fire fighting department. Here, members of the squad prepare to handle a fire emergency, a substantial danger in industrial plants of the time. All of the equipment was manpowered; maintaining horse-drawn equipment may have been judged as impractical for factory purposes.

DISPLAY FOR IMPROVING COUNTY ROADS

The "good roads" movement in the United States began as a coalition of urban bicyclists and farmers in the early 1890s. Many farmers, however, refused to support paving, resisting the added taxes they believed would mainly benefit non-county residents. As a result, county road improvements lagged far behind those of the city, a fact that impacted early automobile design; the Model T, with its high ground clearance and high-torque engine, was designed by Henry Ford to meet the challenge of poor rural roads. This exhibit, sponsored by the Montgomery County commissioners, was designed to attract support for the improvement of county roads.

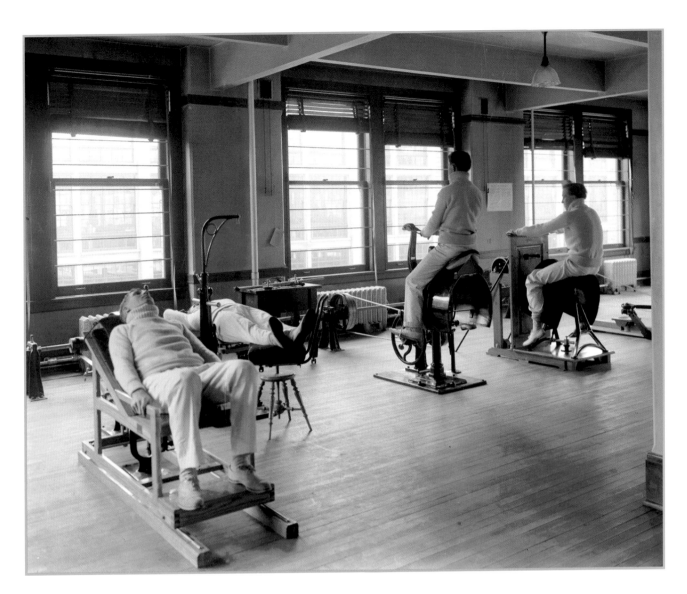

GYMNASIUM, MEN ON EXERCISING MACHINES

As Americans became more health conscious and had more leisure time, they began to develop opportunities for systematic exercise. Gymnasiums were established in many cities, the YMCA being particularly progressive in meeting the need for physical activity. The subject of health was one on which Patterson was most fanatical; as early as 1894 he introduced a twice-daily routine of calisthenics for his women workers and office force. In 1905, he established the Department of Physical Culture, making sure that his employees were taught proper exercise methods. Here, NCR employees work out in the company gymnasium on equipment powered by a belt-drive system similar to that used to run factory machinery.

HOLLOWAY CHILDREN'S HOME, DUNBAR AVENUE

The Holloway Children's Home was a private orphanage operated by Mrs. L. J. Holloway, an African American widow living on Dayton's West Side. She personally assumed the financial burden of operating the institution, said to be home to "scores of orphan children." Little is known about this Dayton philanthropist or her institution, but this home and her farm were the subject of a series of photographs taken by an NCR photographer in the early twentieth century.

FIRE DRILL AT EMERSON SCHOOL, MAY 22, 1912

This photo shows the original Emerson School building, built between Burns Avenue and Hickory Street about 1864. (The current building is now Dayton Christian Middle School). With growing concerns about preventing loss of life in school fires, the city school board added fire escapes to their buildings to provide safe exit in the case of a conflagration. Thus began the practice of holding "fire drills," so that both students and teachers were prepared to act quickly and efficiently in the event of a fire. These students are obviously enjoying trying out their emergency escape route.

CAMP RHOADS, MAY 6, 1913

The flood of March 1913 left large numbers of Daytonians homeless. Many of these refugees were sheltered at Camp Rhoads, located just south of the NCR factory. It was named after Major Thomas Rhoads, who served as an aide to President Woodrow Wilson and who organized the camp. When Governor James M. Cox visited the camp in June, he found a well-equipped and spotlessly clean emergency facility, which he declared to be the "model camp of the world."

GIRLS ENTERING WELFARE HALL, JULY 7, 1905

As part of his program to keep workers healthy and in top notch condition, Patterson established men's and women's dining halls, providing hot, balanced lunches at nominal cost. In 1905, Welfare Hall, an employees' dining room and meeting facility, was erected on Rubicon Street. Built in the typical Patterson way—quickly and efficiently—it was completed in record time, opening on June 20th just twenty days after breaking ground. Practically all the planning and construction was done by the NCR work force.

AUTOMOBILE FIRE TRUCK, HOOK AND LADDER, JANUARY 1922

The development of a modern and efficient fire service was a "must" in a city that prided itself on its progressive management. Dayton's paid fire department was founded in 1864, but remained at the mercy of politicians until it was reestablished on a bipartisan basis in 1880. For many years, the equipment was horse-drawn, but the increasing weight of the new apparatus demanded that horses be replaced by motorized vehicles. The year 1906 is generally seen as the beginning of the motorized fire department in America. Here, firemen pose with one of the city's latest ladder trucks.

WEIGHING THE PUPILS, FRESH AIR CLASS, SECOND GRADE
McKINLEY SCHOOL, PRITZ AND HIGHLAND STREETS

By the early twentieth century, schools were taking a proactive role in protecting and improving children's health. In 1907, medical inspectors were appointed for each city school and a free eye clinic was established. The inspectors served as advisors, examining students and facilities and then issuing recommendations to school authorities. As time passed, stricter regulations were enacted, designed to control the spread of disease among the student population. On January 28, 1914, the City Health Department passed a measure requiring all school children to be vaccinated. In this photograph, a woman weighs children in the Fresh Air Class, which may have been made up of children with special health concerns.

ASSOCIATED CHARITIES, SOUTH JEFFERSON STREET

By the turn of the century, cities were creating centralized agencies to coordinate private philanthropic efforts. Associated Charities was organized on December 20, 1896 during a severe multi-year depression which left 2,000 Dayton men out of work and hundreds of families in need. In 1898, the organization leased this building at 231 South Jefferson Street. In the photo, neatly uniformed matrons provide day care services for children of working parents.

HAWTHORN SCHOOL, SANITARY DRINKING FOUNTAIN

New concerns with providing sanitary conditions for school children prompted the installation of drinking fountains, eliminating the need to share a drinking cup or water dipper. Here, schoolboys demonstrate the ease and convenience of their modern drinking appliance. Hawthorn School, located on McDaniel Street in the McPherson Town neighborhood, was built in 1886.

CRIPPLED CHILDREN'S PUBLIC CLINIC AT BARNEY'S, CIRCA 1921

Barney's Community Center was established in Old North Dayton by Mrs. Harris Gorman, in memory of her grandfather, Eliam E. Barney, and her father, Eugene J. Barney. The Center quickly outgrew its first home in a house at Valley and Chapel Streets, and a new building was constructed on a twelve-acre site on the Mad River. A community center whose mission was concerned with Americanizing the many Eastern European and other immigrants in the neighborhood, it offered a wide range of recreational, educational and social services. The Center was best known, however, for its clinic specializing in the rehabilitation of crippled children. The clinic continued to grow and expand its services; today, it is known as The Children's Medical Center.

WOMAN'S CENTURY CLUB HOUSE FROM THE SOUTH, SEPTEMBER 6, 1906

The Patterson Homestead on Brown Street, completed in 1850, was the boyhood home of John H. Patterson. In July 1904, Patterson announced that he was leasing the home to the NCR Woman's Century Club to use as a meeting center and boarding house for female employees without relatives in the city. Following the usual Patterson method of "better done yesterday than tomorrow," the Company lost no time in making the needed changes. Almost overnight, the house was remodeled, the barn transformed into a modern dormitory and meeting facility, and the famed Olmsted Brothers firm brought in to landscape the grounds. The women assumed management of the facility in September 1904, thus beginning another innovative experiment in worker welfare that was watched and admired by social reformers across the industrial world.

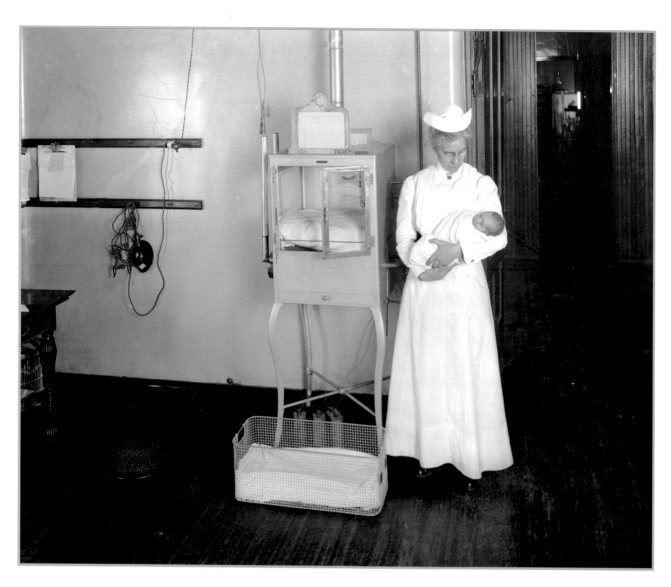

MIAMI VALLEY HOSPITAL MATERNITY WARD, APRIL 2, 1912

Dayton, like many other progressive cities across the country, inaugurated numerous programs to decrease infant mortality rates. Lowering the infant death rate became a particular focus of the new city manager government, which established baby clinics, certified milk stations, and a system of post-natal care. In June 1914, the city manager reported that the death rate for infants was one-half that of any June in the previous three years. Here, a trained nurse holds a young patient in Miami Valley Hospital's maternity ward.

MONTGOMERY COUNTY ORPHANS HOME, MARCH 14, 1912

The care of orphans was managed through private charities until an act passed by the Ohio legislature in 1866 authorizing the establishment of children's homes empowered the Montgomery County commissioners to take charge of the Dayton Orphan Asylum. In 1867, they purchased land on South Summit Street (now South Paul Laurence Dunbar Street), and the new Children's Home was completed and opened the same year. It was the first non-sectarian children's home in the state of Ohio. The care of orphans was one of the first public welfare responsibilities to be assumed by government, setting a pattern that would accelerate as time moved on.

TESTING THE EYE AT ST. ELIZABETH HOSPITAL, DECEMBER 17, 1914

St. Elizabeth, founded in 1878 by the Sisters of the Poor of St. Francis, was Dayton's first permanent hospital. For many years, it was also the city's largest and most progressive facility. St. Elizabeth's Eye, Ear, Nose and Throat Department was established in 1885, and was known for its up-to-date medical techniques and successful corrective procedures. Here, a specialist at the eye clinic provides diagnosis and treatment to city children.

NURSE VISITING A HOME, DECEMBER 9, 1914

The Visiting Nurses Association had its origins in the Fruit and Flower Mission, a private charity founded in 1898 by Dayton society women, who saw the need to provide assistance to those who lacked the services of a hospital or physician. The organization began its district nursing program in 1904. It was incorporated in 1907, and in 1913 became the Visiting Nurses Association. This photo shows a member of the new agency calling on clients at their home.

What ought the Dayton of the future to be?
To become really great,
our city must accomplish the largest amount of good
for the largest number of her citizens,
uniting all the best things which exist in other cities
into an ideal city.

JOHN H. PATTERSON, 1896

——————⟊⟊——————

Every citizen is part of the community.

All must work together for its advancement.

A community spirit is one of the most desirable factors in a prosperous town.

While Dayton may be known as "the city of a thousand factories"

as well as the "most beautiful inland city in the country,"

unless there is a unified interest among the people, unless each feels that the others

are interested in him, and he in the community, we cannot be a real city.

There must be a broad community spirit

where the citizens are not pulling in opposite directions,

but all together for one common purpose.

GREATER DAYTON ASSOCIATION, 1916